DRAGONFLY QIGONG

Dr. Michael Steward Sr.

DRAGONFLY QIGONG

蜻蜓　　氣功

Dragonfly

Oh to be like a dragonfly

Wings always buzzing with excitement

Lovingly caressing the pond of humanity

Then flying upwards towards heaven

When the day is done

By: Dr. Michael Steward Sr.

© Copyright 2003 Michael Steward. All rights reserved.

No part of this publication may be reproduced, stored in a retrieval system, or transmitted, in any form or by any means, electronic, mechanical, photocopying, recording, or otherwise, without the written prior permission of the author.

Advice to the Reader

Before following any type of exercise program, it is recommended that you consult your doctor if you suffer from any health problems, special conditions, or are in any doubt as to its suitability.

```
National Library of Canada Cataloguing in Publication Data

Steward, Michael, 1954-
    Dragonfly qigong / Michael Steward.
ISBN 1-4120-0335-0
    I. Title.
RA781.8.S74 2003           613.7'148                    C2003-902613-2
```

TRAFFORD

This book was published on-demand in cooperation with Trafford Publishing.
On-demand publishing is a unique process and service of making a book available for retail sale to the public taking advantage of on-demand manufacturing and Internet marketing.
On-demand publishing includes promotions, retail sales, manufacturing, order fulfilment, accounting and collecting royalties on behalf of the author.

Suite 6E, 2333 Government St., Victoria, B.C. V8T 4P4, CANADA
Phone   250-383-6864   Toll-free   1-888-232-4444 (Canada & US)
Fax   250-383-6804   E-mail   sales@trafford.com
Web site   www.trafford.com   TRAFFORD PUBLISHING IS A DIVISION OF TRAFFORD HOLDINGS LTD.
Trafford Catalogue #03-0704   www.trafford.com/robots/03-0704.html

DEDICATION

This book is dedicated to all of my students and the continued faith that they have in me, and my teachings. A wise man once said to me, "When a student is ready to learn, a teacher will appear". I think that I am a very lucky man, because I found myself ready to teach and the students appeared.

ACKNOWLEDGEMENTS

I would like to deeply thank my wife Ruth Ann and my daughter Sarah for enduring many hours of watching me sit and type away at the computer creating this book. Their patience and love keep me going everyday. I would like to thank my son Mike for inspiring me to take chances and test the unknown. I want to thank my Mom and Dad for teaching me that, "If you can dream it, then you can achieve it".

I want to thank my top Qigong/Taiji students and great friends, Sifu Patrick Albrecht and (Sifu) Dr. James Barry M.D. for all of their ideas and for all of their help in the development and research into Dragonfly Qigong. Their imaginative and creative minds brought me the new modern tools that make Dragonfly Qigong so unique. I also want to thank them for posing for countless hours while photographing the pictures found in this book.

I want to thank my special friend Bill Douglas, author of several best selling Taiji and Qigong books. Through his leadership by example I was encouraged to write this book.

I want to thank my good friend and devoted student Gayle Shidler, Master-Library Associate at Miami University-Middletown, for taking the time out of her busy schedule to proof read and edit this book.

I want to thank my good friend and devoted student Cristy Carter-Tramell, educational teacher, for her support and help with the technical editing of this book.

I want to thank my good friend and devoted student Robert Carnell, Assistant Professor Miami University, for his support and help with the scientific/technical editing of this book.

Lastly I would like to thank all the special teachers that I have had the opportunity to train with over the years. Through your generous hard work and knowledge you have molded me into the instructor that I am today. Without you I wouldn't have had the desire to continue on and discover what martial arts had to offer me. Thank you for teaching me that it isn't important how much time you have on earth, but what you do with the time that matters.

Thank you most of all for teaching me that to perfect my character, to fulfill my purpose in life, to live up to my fullest potential, I must not allow myself to be held back by imaginary restraints. I must always be willing to try and be willing to try again! You taught me that to become all that I am capable of being; I have to be willing to risk all that I already am. Thank you for showing me that it is this development of strength of character and commitment to continual improvement that will set me apart from everyone else. Xie xie ni!

ABOUT THE AUTHOR:
Dr. Michael Steward Sr.

Ranks & Certifications
- 29 years in the martial arts
- PhD/Martial Arts Sciences/Philosophy
- Master Instructor-Taiji & Qigong
- National Certified U.S.A. Coach
- Inducted Into The World Martial Arts Hall Of Fame 2000
- Inducted Into The World Sports Medicine Hall of Fame 2000
- Inducted Into The World Karate Union Hall Of Fame 2003
- 3 Time Team U.S.A. Member
- American Athletic Trainers Association – Sports Medicine Trainer
- American Sports Medicine Association – Sports Medicine Trainer
- National Qigong Association –Professional Member
- **Personally trained four national champions, twenty-four state champions, five Junior Olympic champions, thirty international USA team members**
- **Personally trained in the following countries; USA, Austria, Germany, Spain, Sweden, Norway, Finland, Ireland, Denmark, Russia, France, and Canada**

Creator of the "Head Smart Body Safe Self-Defense Program" © 1988
Creator of the Ju-Jitsu Weapon System "Raising Some Cane" © 1996
Creator of "Progressive Coaching © 1997
Creator of "Dragonfly Qigong" © 1999

Foreword By; Gayle Shidler

Master-Library Associate-Miami University

Imagine an energy system that explains how we can enjoy better health and improve overall well-being. Imagine practicing an exercise program that will increase energy levels and reduce stress, while strengthening your mind, body and spirit.

Dragonfly Qigong is just such an energy system. Each movement of each exercise promotes health and enhances your personal energy levels, while helping you remain calm and effective in stressful situations.

Dr. Michael Steward's book contains a modern interpretation and presentation of ancient principles and practical exercises that will put those principles into practice in your daily life. Many of the exercises use new materials and techniques to heighten therapeutic changes and awareness. While learning the simple, elegant postures and forms of the ancient Chinese art of Qigong, you will also add a new understanding of universal health.

Studies have shown many positive health benefits will be experienced by anyone practicing Qigong. Some of the conditions which respond with measurable improvement include: back pain; arthritis; cardiovascular conditions, such as hypertension and angina; allergies and digestive problems; asthma and emphysema; dealing with chronic illness; rehabilitation following surgery; recovery from physical injury, such as a sport injury or car accident.

In addition, Qigong has been shown to slow the natural aging process, restore brain functions and have a healing effect - all things which everyone will find beneficial.

The saying "When a student is ready to learn, a teacher will appear" has certainly been true for me. I have studied ancient Chinese philosophy for years, but only recently learned about Qigong. Now, my husband and I are fortunate to take classes with Dr. Michael Steward. Practicing Dragonfly Qigong has added a whole new dimension to our lives. In just two years of practicing and learning the forms and exercises, we have each experienced many positive changes in our physical abilities and mental outlook.

When beginning our lessons in Qigong, my husband had back problems and migraine headaches, which have continued to improve. I began class with lifelong severe arthritis. I have lost weight and several clothing sizes. My blood pressure is now consistently normal, without medication. My posture, muscle tone, flexibility and range of motion have all improved dramatically. I am now able to walk smoothly for miles. My breathing has improved so much that I am learning to sing again with our children and grandchildren.

We are especially grateful to recover the ability to participate in the physical activities we enjoy again. It is clear that the slow movements and graceful forms of Dragonfly Qigong can be practiced by anyone, of any age or physical ability.

Dr. Steward brings extensive knowledge, based on many years of study, practice, teaching and expertise in modern and ancient martial arts, sports health education and Eastern philosophy, to share with us in this excellent and timely volume.

I enthusiastically recommend Dragonfly Qigong!! Practicing Qigong, with this book as your guide, will open the door to a whole new way of strengthening your health and enhancing your quality of life.

Foreword By; Cristy Carter-Tramell
Education Teacher

A Chinese brushstroke is embedded with a history and depth of meaning beyond the simple beauty of what you see. The same can be said of this book and the way Dr. Michael Steward teaches.

I am the student who originally came just to learn a form. Influenced by Dr. Steward's good humor, creative generosity and gentle guidance, I found instead that Taiji/Qigong practice has become an integral part of my life and health - a moving meditation.

And there is so much more I am eager to learn! I was delighted to have an opportunity to read and work on the technical editing of this text. I know this book will encourage and deepen each reader's exploration and understanding of Qigong. Make it your own.

Foreword By; Robert Carnell

Assistant Professor Miami University

My Taiji practice has been a daily investigation of the Tao. No other methods of mind and body self-cultivation can bring one as close to an understanding of the *universal way* as the arts of Qigong and Taiji. If this is your first experience with Qigong, I sincerely hope it is as much an awakening for you.

I was very fortunate to have found Taiji at the early age of twenty. My experience has been that many young people interested in discipline, self defense, and Eastern philosophy choose a harder style of martial arts initially, and then only later in life realize the benefits of this soft and supple art. My academic background is deeply rooted in math, physics, and science, but I have had little trouble with the metaphysical concepts which Taiji/Qigong practitioners espouse. Physics, at its most basic level, is a Taoist discipline. Concepts such as relativity, wave-particle duality, and infinity, which seem difficult for westerners to understand, are more easily fathomed in Taoist terms. Taiji and Qigong exercise is the perfect combination of my medical, scientific, and philosophical views of our world.

Although I have only been a student of Dr. Steward's for a short time, I have learned a great deal. His methods of awakening energy within the body offer a great deal, both to beginning students and to those with long years of practice. Few other schools of Taiji and Qigong can help a novice begin to experience Qi as quickly. My practice has been rejuvenated by and has blossomed from the principles and exercises contained in this book.

I hope that you will enjoy Dr. Steward's teaching as much as I have.

PREFACE/BOOK GOALS

Within the pages of this book I will be discussing the exercises that belong to the Dragonfly Qigong system, and I will be explaining the use of our special modern Qigong tools to enhance these exercises. I will also discuss the new tools aid in an ancient exercise called the Taiji Ruler, which is now called "Dragonfly Thermal Ruler". I will explain the theory of heat transference to the Laogong Point in the palm of your hand, which is located on the pericardium meridian, and the health benefits that are associated with this process. However to address the large and multi-layered subject of Qigong thoroughly, one must explore the hundreds of resources on Qigong that are now widely available.

This book will attempt to uncover and explain one of the many layers of the wondrous benefits of Qigong. The best way however to learn Qigong, of course, is from a personal teacher, one who will guide you as you work with energy. This is especially important for the beginning levels. There is much that can be transmitted from person to person that is all but nearly impossible to get from a video or even a book.

The best way to prove the true effects of Qigong is to simply try it yourself. Its effects will be experienced in your own being. This is much better than taking the word of an author or even a teacher. Try it yourself and see what it does to your own energy. As you move deeper into your own personal practice, you will be more and more able to track the changes in your life that Qigong will produce. I hope you enjoy this book and all the benefits it offers for your exploration into Qigong.

CONTENTS PAGE

DEDICATION...II

ACKNOWLEDGEMENTS.................................III

ABOUT THE AUTHOR......................................VI

FOREWARDS..VII

PREFACE/GOALS OF THIS BOOK.....................XV

CONTENTS..XVII

EXPLORING THE WONDERS & BENEFITS OF QIGONG (CHAPTER 1)...Page 1

THE EVOLUTION OF THE NAME DRAGONFLY QIGONG (CHAPTER 2)...Page 19

THE TRADITIONAL CHINESE MEDICINE CONCEPT OF HUMAN ENERGY FLOW (CHAPTER 3)...Page 23

THE PERICARDIUM MERIDIAN & THE LAOGONG POINT

(CHAPTER 4)...Page 31

THERMAL HEAT TRANSFER SCIENTIFIC THEORY

(CHAPTER 5)...Page 40

SOMETHING OLD AND SOMETHING NEW, SOMETHING BORROWED SOMETHING BLUE

(CHAPTER 6)...Page 48

IMAGERY AND VISUALIZATION

(CHAPTER 7)...Page 61

DRAGONFLY QIGONG EXERCISES

(CHAPTER 8)...Page 69

DRAGONFLY THERMAL RULER EXERCISES

(CHAPTER 9)...Page 122

CONCLUSION..Page 199

Exploring the Wonders and Benefits of Qigong

Qi

Gong

      The term Qigong (chee gong) is made of two characters. It is the basic life force of the universe; it is what animates us, what warms us, keeps our organs in their places and directs all of our movements. The first character Qi means energy. Qi as the golden thread that unites our body, mind and spirit, the link between what is happening inside our bodies, and what is taking place outside our bodies. The western medical society is only now appreciating the long established health virtues of Qigong. Researchers worldwide are bringing a scientific understanding to Traditional Chinese Medicine and Chinese Health Systems.

The second character gong means work or exercise. Thus, the term Qigong means working with, or exercising your energy. Qigong is a series of movements or exercises, both internal and external that will directly activate and facilitate a smooth flow of Qi/Chi or vital force throughout the body.

There are many different types of Qigong, some quite vigorous and some sublimely simple. Effects will vary, according to the skill level of the practitioner, the consistency of the practice, his or her age and relative health. No matter what style you choose, however, all Qigong deals with accessing, circulating and storing Qi, or vital force, within the body. Strengthening and building the body's Qi (Chi) has been the concept preoccupying seekers of health in China for centuries. In traditional Chinese medicine the flow of energy Qi along channels or meridians in the body is viewed as central to a person's health and well-being, with illness being attributed to restricted or blocked Qi flow within the body. This concept provides the basis for acupuncture, acupressure and Qigong. The ability to build and direct the Qi flow in your body will enhance your health and reduce the chance of illness.

For thousands of years people in China have developed, refined and practiced successfully the art of building Qi. Qigong is an integral component of Chinese health systems.

The beginnings of energy exercises can be traced to Huang Ti, the Yellow Emperor who ruled around 2700 BCE. He is said to have practiced a form of exercise called Dao Yin. Dao means to guide and Yin means to lead. Dao Yin, still practiced today, is a set of prescribed movements, some spinal twists and stretches and other polarity or energy balancing movements, which help to open up the Qi meridians in the body and allows for smoother and stronger flow of energy.

In those days Qigong was based primarily on movements learned by observing animals in nature. Arm exercises, for example, were drawn from the manner in which birds flap their wings; leg exercises imitated a tiger's gait, shoulder postures were learned from watching bears, and so forth.

As various forms of movement exercises were developed over history, they were passed down through several different families, each jealously guarding their secret practices, until they eventually became common knowledge.

Qigong is not just about moving your body in elegant circles. It is about being able to tap into the very flow of the universe, the movement of energy as it flows through your being, and as it is expressed by you personally. Each movement in Dragonfly Qigong is designed to move the energy into your meridians and through your body, each in a very precise manner. In the beginning, it is very important to understand the basic principles of Qigong and to be able to build upon them so that your practice becomes a manifestation of your own personal energy system. To force yourself to move in a way that is unnatural for you is a waste of time and can even be dangerous. Find a teacher who can pass on the principles and the postures in such a way that you can make them your own, through practice, through perseverance, and through a discovery of your own nature. Then you can find your own expression of Qigong.

It is a wonderful way to learn how to maintain our body, mind and spirit within the often times challenging everyday situations of life. By learning how to keep a calm and balanced center while moving from side to side and sometimes walking, we can learn how to maintain a sense of balance and a sense of being centered in the rest of our lives.

Qigong exercises can help you settle into the experience of your body and your surroundings and re-establish contact with what is happening now. You need to make your Qigong practice an integral part of your life by applying the lessons you learn to your daily experience. Qigong can help us learn to respond to life in a balanced and harmonious way, using the yin/yang energies in a flowing and spontaneous manner. We can use Qigong to discover in our own lives, how to be open to change and growth, and the miracle of life unfolding all around us in a great circular and ever changing world we live in. Just like the dragonfly emerges from a larvae stage into a beautiful winged creature, we too can develop the energies needed to cope with the world around us, and to become healthier human beings.

As mentioned earlier, the art of Qigong requires hard work and perseverance.

Significant changes cannot be brought about in a single day. It takes time to reroute the often times unnatural flows of Qi that has built up in our bodies. It can take years of practice to heal long lasting health problems, or to build up enough vital Qi so that new health problems do not occur. It can take a lifetime of practice to be able to align one's Qi with the Qi of the universe, and be able to transcend the physical world, as we know it, at the Point of death or before. But all along the way there are rewards and great health benefits for anyone who pursues a regular practice.

The positive results can be of a physical nature, or emotional, psychological, spiritual or a combination of all four. Practicing Qigong will make you healthier, more emotionally centered, more psychologically balanced, more creative, happier, and stress free. It will strengthen your will; deepen your character, and much more. This may seem unbelievable, but it is indeed true. Long-term regular practice of any kind of Qigong can produce all of these results and more.

"Practice regularly and maintain" might very well be that single most important principle.

If you can practice regularly and maintain your practice, you will develop a basis of strong discipline, which is often the door that leads to energy growth.

When you maintain your practice, your knowledge about the principles of Qigong will deepen, your sensitivity and understanding of energy will deepen, and you will experience many challenges and insights. With the proper teacher, the techniques act simultaneously as a mirror that will allow us to see ourselves, and help us to improve.

Stopping too soon is one of the biggest mistakes that newcomers to Qigong make. They are all too often in search of a quick fix, figuring they will do Qigong for a month or so and they will be "fixed", that they will be taken care of, or that they will have received all that Qigong has to offer at that point. They want Qigong to be an external solution, which will cause some change without their participation. They expect that they won't have to take part in the process, that Qigong will do it all by itself. They don't want to be present, they just want the fix. They don't seem to get the idea that Qigong is a process that requires presence and vitality, active cooperation in the process, and time.

Some people stop because they just can't see the value of what Qigong is offering. They stop before catching the idea, before realizing that Qigong is an inner awareness process. Often such people refuse to accept that such an approach to awareness exists. Sometimes, even if they experience the inner awareness, they cannot fathom the importance the inner awareness will have on their lives.

Stressing quality over quantity of repetitions in your practice is helpful. In the long run, correct technique is more important than the outcome. It also helps to not allow negative habits to get started. If we allow negative habits or the pull toward laziness, the negative habits will win regularly and settle into place. This will cause your practice and growth to be inhibited. It is best to not to skip practice, but to practice every day without fail. For once negative habits get started, your energy will cease to flow smoothly, and it will become even harder to get started again. However, if you practice regularly, your energy will remain active and vibrant and your spirit can remain lively, which should in turn make practice fluid, interesting, and enjoyable.

Keeping your energy raised, with a sense of curiosity, and vitality is a key ingredient for making daily practice work.

Remember, Qigong is more the underlying principles than simply the postures. It is the principles that make the postures and energies of Qigong what they should be. The way to achieve full energy potential is to carefully and intensely study the principles. Take nothing for granted, and investigate for yourself what the principles truly mean. Though there are numerous classics and master's commentaries, you must remain vital and alive and apply your best efforts toward understanding the principles directly and for yourself.

One of the basic things that Qigong offers is beauty. It brings us together with that silent inner craving which exists in all of us, the hunger to touch beauty. Whether, the beauty lies in the flowing fluidity of the Qigong movements, in the sense of history, in the remarkable esthetic "look" of the postures, in the wonderful feeling of harmony, in the simplicity, in the incredible harmoniousness which Qigong evokes, in the power, or in the extraordinary feeling which its slowness and mindfulness brings, that beauty is there. It is available to any practitioner who can accept the subtle realm and who practices regularly and maintains in practice. Practicing regularly and maintaining is the principle that makes it work.

"Inner and outer harmony"
What you practice, you become!

Every day extensive research is being conducted in China, and in various parts of the world, on the effects of Qigong practice. One of the most important discoveries was that the nervous condition of the sympathetic stress reaction relaxed greatly and sympathetic impulses decreased. This indicates relaxation. This continued to a decrease of the following: arterial pressure, cellular metabolic rates, blood sugar concentration, and mental activity, and also relaxed muscular tones. After longer periods of practice, mental relaxation, ability to cope with stress, improved sleep, and a general energy increase were noted.

Qigong is used regularly in hospitals all over China for the treatment of heart disease and cancer as well as for many other illnesses. All Qigong practice concerns accessing, circulating and storing Qi as well as directing, enhancing and building a strong current of Qi in the body. The various Qi pathways in the body range from major meridians such as the Du Mai (flows up the back), the Ren Mai (flows down the front), Dai Mai the belt channel (flows around the waist), the Chong Mai (flows directly through the center of the body), the major yin channels (flow along the inside of the arms and legs), and the major yang channels (flow along the outside of the arms and legs).

Along those pathways are certain points that are used to either access or enhance the Qi in that area. Several important points often used in Qigong practice are the Bai Hui point at the top of the head (the heaven's gate), the Tian Mu point between the eyebrows (the third eye), the Shan Zhong point (the heart center), the Wei Lu point at the bottom of the sacrum, the Hui yin point on the perineum, the Yongquan (bubbling well) Point at the bottoms of the feet, and the points we are concerned with in this book, the Laogong (labor palace) Points on the palms of the hands. When these points are energized and "opened," the Qi in the pathways can run smoother and stronger.

There are also three major energy reservoirs or dantians in the body. Dan means medicine or elixir and tian means field. The top dantian is the third eye area, including the pineal gland. The middle dantian is the heart area around the solar plexus.

The lower dantian is three finger widths below the navel. All of these areas are located inside of the body, rather than on the surface. As with the points, once these areas are stimulated and energized the amount of Qi available to the practitioner grows immensely.

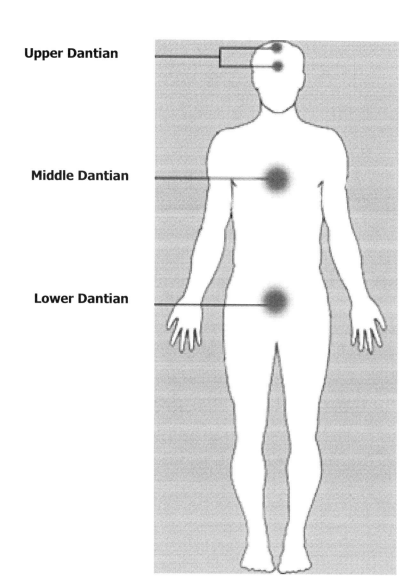

Three Dantians or Three Treasures

Qigong also works with the Qi field that is located both inside and outside the body. Passing the hands down the front or back of the body can affect one's internal organs because of the relationship between the outer and inner Qi field.

As humans we are a fulcrum between heavenly energy and earthly energy. A strong electromagnetic field produced by the planets and stars in the heavens exerts a powerful influence upon us, and the electromagnetic power of the earth itself also exerts a strong influence upon us. We receive heavenly energy through our Bai Hui Point at the very top of the head; we receive earthly energy through our Yongquan Point at the bottoms of our feet, which are the beginning of the kidney channel, also called the Bubbling Well Point. When we work with "opening" and energizing these points, we are better able to be a clear channel for heavenly and earthly energy, both for our own health and to be able to heal others. That combined with the unimpeded circulation of Qi in our bodies makes us strong vital beings.

Qigong practice, which combines deep and regular breathing, slow movements and correct visualization, can have a profound effect on our entire existence. The psycho-physiological effect of performing soft, slow movements in conjunction with deep diaphragmatic breathing is to switch the autonomous nervous system over from the chronically overactive sympathetic mode to the calming, restorative parasympathetic mode, in which the body's various vital functions and energies are balanced, harmonized, and secretions of vital essence such as hormones and neuro-chemicals are stimulated.

There is an old saying that "Qi follows Yi," meaning that Qi can be directed by the mind. Ancient practitioners of Qigong knew what modern western medical science is only discovering, that we can direct healing energy with our mind and affect the healing process. Experiments have been conducted in which practitioners send energy to a certain part of their bodies; that area is then measured with heat sensitive instruments. Results have shown an increase in heat radiation in the area to where the practitioner has directed Qi. In the beginning stages of Qigong practice we use our minds to gently guide or lead Qi through the pathways and through the points we are working with. In the higher stages of practice we cease even using the mind, simply letting the Qi guide itself.

Qigong practice not only aligns our own body/mind/spirit but also aligns us with the universal body/mind/spirit. By regulating our minds through meditation and gentle movement we can facilitate a smoother and stronger flow of energy throughout our bodies, giving us greater health and freedom of movement throughout our lives.

Qigong is actually an approach to life itself. It is a state of mind characterized by complete relaxation and complete acceptance, deep meditation and love, joy and beneficence, renewal and rebirth; it is open to the healing energy of the universe, and it offers healing for the whole world.

Qigong is a way to access the energy of the universe and make it our own. It is a way to help our own internal energy flow smoothly and strongly throughout our bodies. It is a way to open our spiritual eyes to be able to see beyond what our physical eyes can reach. It is an exchange on a deep and basic level of our inner being and with that exchange comes balance, harmony, composure of spirit, deepening of character, relaxing of mind and muscles, of being empty and full at the same time, of being attentive to detail, clear of vision, open hearted, soft yet strong, like water, like wind, like the heat of the sun, sensitive to changes in the energetic atmosphere, and openness to change, transformation and miracles.

THE EVOLUTION OF THE NAME DRAGONFLY QIGONG

Over the past 20 years I have modified some very ancient forms of Taiji Ball and Taiji Golden Ruler exercises into their present modern forms called Dragonfly Qigong. I have also replaced the old style tools that we had been using like the wooden/steel ball and wooden/steel ruler, with the new neoprene "Thermal Ball" and the closed cell foam hollow core "Thermal Rulers". I struggled however with the task of finding a name for my Qigong exercises for several months. I needed a name that would reflect the special heat manipulation properties of the new exercises and new tools.

One day while I was sitting on a bench gazing at my oriental water garden, a dragonfly touched down and landed on my knee. I was contemplating the Qigong system that I had developed at the time, and what name I would give it. You might say that I found my spirit guide that day, within the beauty of that dragonfly.

After a little research into dragonflies, my task of finding a name became instantly easier. Destiny had taken me by the hand. Heat is the dragonfly's main catalyst for metamorphosis or change in growth, from larvae through adulthood. The Dragonfly has an addiction to heat.

Figure 1-Prehistoric Dragonfly Fossil

In the prehistoric jungles of some 300 million years ago, when trees were towering giants, dragonflies as big as hawks soared through the air. We know this because their prehistoric remains have been found in the Permian rocks of Kansas, in the Jurassic formations of Siberia and many other parts of the world. With wings nearly thirty inches from tip to tip, they were the largest insects that ever lived.

Dragonflies were one of the earliest insect forms to appear on earth. The dragonfly has lived on as a creature from the distant past to this day, even while the dinosaurs passed into oblivion and cavemen evolved into modern man. The only thing that has changed about the dragonfly is its size.

The dragonfly is very much a creature of the air and of the sun. In the air, a dragonfly is as graceful as a ballet dancer, while it swoops, turns, and zooms about at will. It can dive like a small plane, or hover like a helicopter, as long as the sun is shining.

Most dragonflies need the sun to fly, and will alight even when the sun goes behind a cloud for even a few minutes. The transformation from underwater nymph to dragonfly is amazing. Its metamorphosis takes place in the heat of the day.

Dragonflies are reminders that we are light and can reflect the light in powerful ways if we choose to do so. "Let there be light" is the divine prompting to use the creative imagination as a force within your life. They help you to see through your illusions and allow your own light to shine in a new vision.

The dragonfly symbolizes going past self-created illusions that limit our growing and changing. Dragonflies are a symbol of the sense of self that comes with maturity.

The Traditional Chinese Medicine Concept of Human Energy Flow

Many cultures define health and illness in the framework of the flow of vital energy through the body. Illness is believed to result when the flow of energy is not in balance or is interfered with. Traditional Chinese Medicine views illness as an imbalance of two types of energy, yin and yang, which simultaneously exist in everyone and everything and within each other.

The practice of movement and breathing exercises known as Qigong is used to build one's life force, and give one the ability to have control over the energy's flow.

The traditional conception of energy flow is the stimulation of points by external or internal methods. The body is made up of meridians consisting of groups of these points. The meridians are divided into yin or yang (negative and positive), and finally, the further division of the meridians into a five-element classification.

The flow of Qi through the body is by way of the meridian system composed of acupuncture points, also known as pressure points. The electrical conductance of skin at acupuncture points is normally high. Since there are several hundred acupuncture points, Traditional Chinese Medicine has classified them into twelve main groups and a few subsidiary ones, with each being assigned a relation to a particular organ function. The energy is seen to flow from the ground up the front of the body and down the back, with the front being yin and the back, yang. The twelve meridians in the order of energy flow, along with their corresponding element and yin or yang state are the following:

Organ	**Element**	**State**
Lungs	Metal	Yin
Large Intestine	Metal	Yang
Stomach	Earth	Yang
Spleen	Earth	Yin
Heart	Fire	Yin
Small Intestine	Fire	Yang
Bladder	Water	Yang
Kidney	Water	Yin
Pericardium	Fire	Yin
Triple Warmer	Fire	Yang
Gall Bladder	Wood	Yang
Liver	Wood	Yin

All of these are bilateral and occur on both sides of the body. Eight additional meridians serve us as "energy reservoirs". They are very important for distributing energy to the other meridians. These eight extraordinary vessels act as Qi reservoirs and thus, do not have a set flow pattern. One of their main functions is to supply or balance the twelve meridians with Qi when any one of them has a shortage, as well as to drain off or sedate Qi when any of them has an excess amount of Qi. Due to this functionality they have to be able to distribute Qi flow in different directions.

The pericardium is a protective sheath around the heart and the triple warmer is a functional energy system involved in regulating the activities of the other organs. There is a distinctive pattern of two organs with the same element designation, but opposite yin-yang "charges". There is a circular flow of energy that proceeds via a yin-yin (negative to negative) to yang-yang (positive to positive) cycle. This is known as the diurnal cycle and the flow moves from one organ to another every two hours.

DAILY MERIDIAN CYCLE

12 Noon

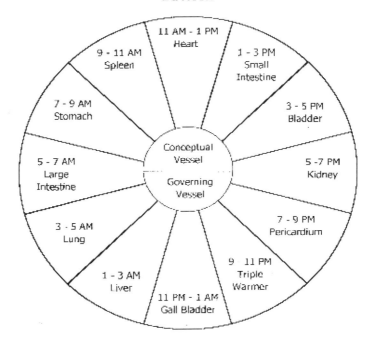

Midnight

Meridian Channels Time Chart

1. Shuigou Xue during the time of the Rat (11 p.m. – 1 a.m.)-Gall Bladder

2. Dianyan Xue during the time of the Ox (1-3 a.m.)-Liver

3. Jiaogong Xue during the time of the Tiger (3-5 a.m.)-Lungs

4. Zisai Xue during the time of the Rabbit (5-7 a.m.)-Large Intestines

5. Daiying Xue during the time of the Dragon (7-9 a.m.)-Stomach

6. Jiagdai Xue during the time of the Snake (9-11 a.m.)-Spleen

7. Maiguan Xue during the time of the Horse (11 a.m. – 1 p.m.)-Heart

8. Jigan Xue during the time of the Ram (1-3 p.m.)-Small Intestines

9. Xuanhai Xue during the time of the Monkey (3-5 p.m.)-Bladder

10. Baihai Xue during the time of the Cock (5-7 p.m.)-Kidney

11. Donghudilou Xue during the time of the Dog (7-9 p.m.)-Pericardium/Heat Governor

12. Yongquan Xue during the time of the Boar (9-11 p.m.)-Triple Warmer/Heater

As a disciple of martial arts we were always taught how to use the vital points and energy meridians to heal before we were allowed to use them for self-defense. The healing aspects of the 12 meridians are well documented in medical and physical Chinese history. By practicing corresponding Qigong exercises with the right meridians you heighten the medical benefits of the exercise.

Acupuncture points have certain electrical properties, and stimulating these points alters chemical neurotransmitters in the body. Breathing and movement exercises to build and control Qi have been developed, and have great therapeutic benefits. These exercises are known as "Qigong" or "Chee Kung" in Chinese. Breathing is the most important aspect of this art. Qigong is defined as the manipulation of vital energy, and has been practiced in China for thousands of years. It is based on the premise that Qi, or vital energy, is a life force, which runs throughout the body and can be developed and directed by Qigong exercises. The cure of disease is due to the effects of Qi, which under the influence of mind conduction, flows along the meridians and attacks the diseased site. Qi also operates systematically to moderate the human body's immune functions. Dragonfly Qigong stimulates several of the most important gateways of energy in our bodies, especially the Laogong Points in the palms of the hands.

THE PERICARDIUM MERIDIAN & THE LAOGONG POINT

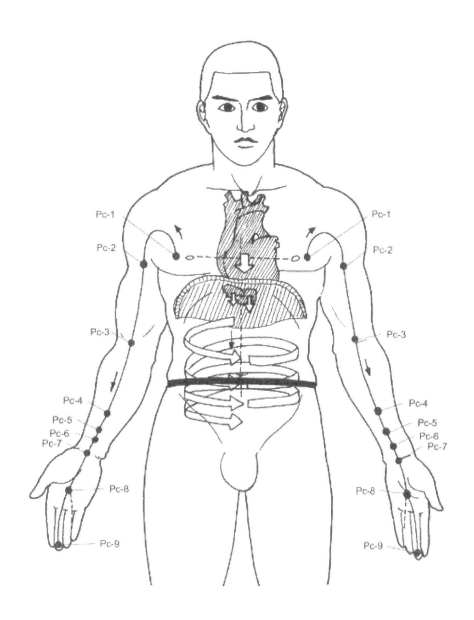

PERICARDIUM MERIDIAN
Fire, Yin

Pericardium Meridian

The pericardium (Yin) and the triple burner (Yang) are paired organs. They are said to correspond to the "Ministerial Fire," as opposed to the "Sovereign Fire" of the heart and small intestine. Though the pericardium has no separate physiological functions, it is generally mentioned with regard to the delirium induced by high fevers.

The regulation of Qi in the pericardium is considered a very important subject in Qigong. It is believed that the heart, the most vital organ in your body, must have a proper level of Qi circulation in order to function normally. The Qi level of the heart can be raised easily to an abnormal state by illness, emotional disturbance, exercise, or injury. The function of the pericardium is to dissipate the excess Qi from the heart and direct it to the Laogong cavity (PC-8) located in the center of the palm. From Laogong, the excess Qi will be released naturally, and hence, regulate the heart's Qi level. The Laogong cavity is used in Qigong massage to reduce the body's temperature during a fever. You can see that the purpose of the pericardium is to regulate the Qi in the heart through the Laogong cavity.

QIGONG AND OUTSIDE GATES

It is important to understand that in Qigong it is believed that there are five centers (called gates) where the Qi of the body is able to communicate with the surrounding environment, and, consequently, regulate the Qi level in your body.

In the human body Qi travels along 12 main meridians; along these meridians are acupuncture points. Five of these points are gates connecting the body to the outside.

1. **Yintang**, the mid-point between the eyebrows.
2. **Bai Hui**, at the top of the head centered between the ears.
3. **Laogong**, middle of palm between third finger and fourth fingers.
4. **Yongquan**, mid line of bottom of foot about 1/3 distance from toes.
5. **Mingmen**, located opposite dantian in small of back; this is also called the life gate.

The lower dantian, which is located two inches below the

navel is the centrally important Qi warehouse. However, the dantian does not exist along a meridian and is not considered an outside gate. In Qigong practice the mind needs to focus on one of these five gates.

Manipulation

The polarity that swings the planets in their orbits through the universe also works on a microcosmic level in the body. In this body energy field there are charges of positive energy (activity); negative energy (receptivity), and neutral energy (balance).

In general, the head is positive, the feet are negative and the joints are neutral. The left hand is negative and receives energy. The right hand is positive and projects energy. The thumb is neutral and relates to the wood element. The index finger is negative and relates to the air element. The middle finger is positive and relates to the fire element. The ring finger is negative and relates to the water element. The little finger is positive and relates to the earth element. By placing a positive hand or finger on a negative part of the body an energy flow takes place.

Benefits

According to theory, "Laogong" Point *(Palace of Labor / Pericardium-8)* at the center of the palm can attract earth (yin) energy when the palms face the ground. This energy is thought to nourish, invigorate and regulate the blood. Conversely, when the palms turn up, they can absorb heavenly (yang) energy, increasing the vital energy of the body. With diligent practice of the "Dragonfly Qigong" exercise, blood circulation should improve and yin and yang energy will come into closer balance.

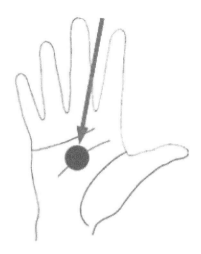

PC 8: LAOGONG (Labor's Palace)

Lao means labor and gong means center. The hand is for labor, so here Lao refers to the hand. The point in the center of the palm is a fire and yin point. When this point is struck, it heats the heart. When used in healing, it cools the heart. This point is known as the point where the Qi emanates from, either for healing, or for martial arts application. This is where the Qi comes from when we put out either healing Qi or disruptive Qi. The hand can be open or closed, it doesn't matter, and energy or Qi still comes from this point. It can also be used as a 'balancing' point for when we do 'meridian balancing' on someone to balance the yin/yang energy in the body. The PC8 point on the left hand is held over the 'earth' point on each meridian.

Then the other PC8 point on the right hand is rubbed down the length of the meridian.

The Hands: The Movable Zone

The hands have some special functions in Qigong. Of the five zones or gates, the hands have the role of magnifying energies in and around them. They do this through actions of picking up and pulling back, expanding outward and condensing inward, in the region of the zones. They can also move energies up and down through the zones, along the meridians, either through a general magnetizing effect or actual projection into Qi gates.

The hands are windows into the entire practice of Qigong. The powers of giving and receiving, initiating contact and expression, so important in Qigong, are seen clearly in them. In this sense the hands act as extensions of the organism, magnifying and amplifying spiritual realities as a projected center. These centers (the hands) revolve and pivot in relation to the greater centers of the torso and head. Within themselves the hands open and close, expanding and condensing around the center, the Laogong Point (Labor Palace).

Developing Qi energy flow involves allowing Qi energy, the collection of all the energies in the body responsible for its general maintenance, repair, balance and well being, to flow without obstruction.

How can we generate Qi/Energy?

The question of how to generate Qi energy lies surprisingly, in not what action you take, but in the Taoist concept of 'non-action." The first step is to find a way that allows our body to function naturally without interference.

Calming the mind is an essential self-discipline when learning how to generate Qi energy. A tranquil mind allows the body to find its own natural balance and any excess energy to sink to a lower position in the body for storage.

The main energizing center for the body's basic energy system is located in the lower abdomen. When this energy center is balanced and functioning correctly, it can generate enormous amounts of energy that can vitalize, invigorate and cleanse all activity within the body.

SCIENTIFIC THEORY-THERMAL DYNAMICS OF HEAT TRANSFER USING NEW-AGE TOOLS

The human body is in reality an energy system. You can even think of the body's meridians as an electrical system, complete with junctions, fuse boxes and miles of wiring, all connecting up in one great multi-dimensional energy circuit. Dragonfly Qigong utilizes the manipulation of heat/energy in the Laogong Points on the palms of the hands, thus completing the electrical circuit and allowing the free flow of energy.

Heat Transfer

The transfer of heat is normally from a high temperature object to a lower temperature object. Heat transfer changes the internal energy of both systems involved according to the First Law of Thermodynamics.

The First Law of Thermodynamics is the application of the conservation of energy principle to heat and thermodynamic processes.

First Law of Thermodynamics

The change in internal energy of a system is equal to the heat added to the system minus the work done by the system.

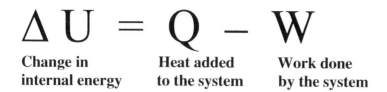

Change in internal energy   **Heat added to the system**   **Work done by the system**

The first law makes use of the key concepts of internal energy, heat, and system work.

Internal Energy

Internal energy is defined as the energy associated with the random, disordered motion and vibration of molecules. It is separated in scale from the macroscopic ordered energy associated with moving objects; it refers to the invisible microscopic energy on the atomic and molecular scale.

Kinetic Energy

Kinetic energy is energy of motion. The kinetic energy of an object is the energy it possesses because of its motion. The kinetic energy of a point mass m with linear velocity v is given by;

Kinetic Energy = ½ mv²

Kinetic energy quantifies the amount of work the object could do as a result of its motion. The total mechanical energy of an object is the sum of its kinetic energy and potential energy. Potential energy is the energy derived from an object's position in a force field (i.e. gravity) in relation to some reference.

For an object of finite size, this kinetic energy is called the translational kinetic energy of the mass, to distinguish it from any rotational kinetic energy it might possess. The total kinetic energy of a mass can be expressed as the sum of the translational kinetic energy of its center of mass plus the kinetic energy of rotation about its center of mass.

Temperature

An operational definition of temperature is that it is a measure of the average translational kinetic energy associated with the disordered microscopic motion of atoms and molecules. The details of the relationship to molecular motion are described in kinetic theory. The temperature defined from kinetic theory is called the kinetic temperature. Temperature is not directly proportional to internal energy since temperature measures only the translational kinetic energy part of the internal energy, so two objects with the same temperature do not in general have the same internal energy. Temperatures are measured in one of the three standard temperature scales (Celsius, Kelvin, and Fahrenheit).

Basics of Heat Transfer

In simplest terms, the discipline of heat transfer is concerned with only two things: temperature and the flow of heat. Temperature represents the amount of thermal energy available, whereas heat flow represents the movement of thermal energy from place to place.

On a microscopic scale, thermal energy is related to the kinetic energy of molecules. The greater a material's temperature, the greater the thermal agitation of its constituent molecules (manifested both in linear motion and vibrational modes). It is natural for regions containing greater molecular kinetic energy to pass this energy to regions with less kinetic energy.

Several material properties serve to modulate the heat transferred between two regions at differing temperatures. Examples include thermal conductivities, specific heats, material densities, fluid velocities, surface emissivities, and more. Taken together, these properties serve to make the solution of many heat transfer problems into an involved process.

Heat Transfer Mechanisms

Heat transfer mechanisms can be grouped into three broad categories:

Conduction: Regions with greater molecular kinetic energy will pass their thermal energy to regions with less molecular energy through direct molecular collisions, a process known as conduction.

Convection: When heat conducts into a static fluid it leads to a local volumetric expansion. Such heat-induced fluid motion in initially static fluids is known as free convection.

Radiation: All materials radiate thermal energy in amounts determined by their temperature, in relation to their environment, where the energy is carried by photons of light in the infrared and visible portions of the electromagnetic spectrum. When temperatures are uniform, the radiative flux between objects is in equilibrium and no net thermal energy is exchanged. The balance is upset when temperatures are not uniform, and thermal energy is transported from surfaces of higher to surfaces of lower temperature.

Important factors for my theory on Dragonfly Qigong:

Radiation heat transfer is concerned with the exchange of thermal radiation energy between two or more bodies. Thermal radiation is defined as electromagnetic radiation in the wavelength range of 0.1 to 100 microns (which encompasses the visible light spectrum), and arises as a result of a temperature difference between two bodies.

No medium need exist between the two bodies for radiative heat transfer to take place (as is needed by conduction and convection), but the introduction of closed cell foam and neoprene rubber products will enhance the heat transfer results.

The heat transferred into or out of an object by thermal radiation is a function of several components. These include its surface reflectivity, emissivity, surface area, temperature, and geometric orientation with respect to other thermally participating objects. In turn, an object's surface reflectivity and emissivity is a function of its surface conditions (roughness, finish, etc.) and composition.

SOMETHING OLD, SOMETHING NEW
SOMETHING BORROWED, SOMETHING BLUE

> **"We borrow from the past,
> to change the present,
> and enhance the future".**

Dr. Michael Steward Sr.

The above quote holds true in every aspect of human life. Dragonfly Qigong has also utilized this theory of evolution by engaging the use of modern tools in our exercises. I have borrowed from the ancient exercises of Taiji Ball and Taiji Ruler, and incorporated the new modern tools consisting of neoprene rubber and closed cell hollow core foam rods, to cut down the time that it would have taken originally to experience the benefits in health. With the old tools made of wood and steel it might have taken the practitioner several months, to a lifetime of practice in order to engage the complete benefits of these exercises. Now with the use of neoprene and closed cell foam tools we can feel the results almost instantly.

The heat and energy produced by the new modern thermal tools, and the adapted ancient exercises, allows us to completely manipulate the Laogong Points in the palms of the hands. This action unblocks the special gates in the palm of the hands, thus allowing the practitioner to dissipate the excess Qi and heat from the heart and direct it to the Laogong cavity located in the center of the palm. From the Laogong Points, the excess Qi will be released naturally and hence, regulate the heart's Qi level. This in turn will help lower the stress level of the practitioner and it will also aid in the healing of hypertension, and high blood pressure.

Humans have electric impulses produced by the heart, brain, and muscles. The body produces light, magnetic fields, and chemical actions. These energies relate to Qi. In slow circular actions they become magnetic fields.

The body also produces heat, which is constantly in movement from one Point to another. This energy travels along meridians. There are several theories on the movement of Qi through the body. Some believe that it moves through the space between the muscle tissues, while others hold that it travels along the small veins.

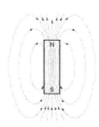
Dragonfly Qigong exercises sensitizes the hands to the presence of the body's electromagnetic field. When your two hands are held parallel to each other they behave the same as two poles of a bar magnet. Electrical lines of force can be felt traveling from one hand to the other and so too can the magnetic fields surrounding them.

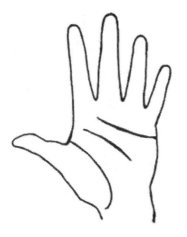 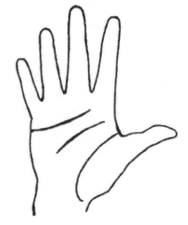

Left Hand Negative   **Right Hand Positive**

For many years we have used and depended on the ancient tools of Taiji Ball and Taiji Ruler. These tools were either made of porous lightweight wood or steel. Thanks to a couple of my ingenious students we have utilized new modern materials that expedite the healing benefits of these ancient exercises. This chapter will introduce you to these two students, Sifu Patrick Albrecht, and (Sifu) Dr. James Barry M.D. This chapter will tell you the stories behind their discoveries. The chapter will also tell you how to make the thermal rulers and where to purchase or find the thermal ball.

DRAGONFLY'S SPECIALIZED TOOLS

Figure 2-Old Style Tai-Qi Wooden Ball 5, 6, or 12" in diameter-made of light weight porous wood or hollow core steel

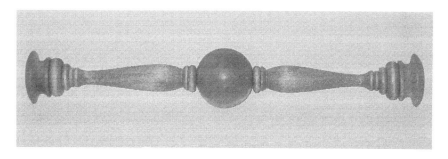

Figure 3-Old Style Taiji Wooden Ruler 8, 10, 12, or 14" in length-made of light weight porous wood or steel

Figure 4-New Thermal Ball/Neoprene Rubber Ball

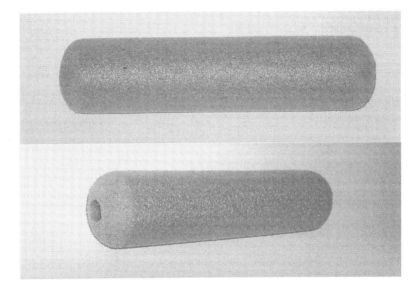

Figure 5-New Thermal Ruler/Closed Cell Hollow Core Foam

Dragonfly Qigong utilizes the heat generated from the Laogong Points in the palm of the hands. These exercises are now super-charged with new modern tools.

Our Thermal Rulers are made from buoyant, lightweight, unique closed cell polyethylene foam. This is the typical swimming pool noodle. The Water Noodle is a popular and versatile exercise tool that provides buoyant support for suspended water exercise and increased resistance for enhanced upper body conditioning. The noodle is hollow and is made of premium quality Ethafoam. Ethafoam is inert polyethylene that is easy to cut and shape and conforms to preservation standards. You can find these noodles at www.thepooltoystore.com, a great pool supply store. You simply cut the thermal tubes to the desired length (8, 10, or 12"), and then use a disc sander to round off the edges. By rounding the end of the tubes you allow a more comfortable fit in the palm of the hands.

Our Thermal Ball is made of Neoprene Rubber (Polychloroprene) and is noted for a unique combination of properties, which has led to its use in thousands of applications in diverse environments. It is the product which skin diving wetsuits are made of. You can purchase these balls at most department stores.

For perhaps the first time, closed cell polyethylene foam (Thermal Ruler) and neoprene rubber (Thermal Ball) can be used with confidence in conjunction with Qigong, to amplify the results.

The ancient Qigong exercises known as Taiji-Ball and Taiji Golden Ruler have taken a giant leap into the 21st Century with Dragonfly Qigong. Through the utilization of special closed cell foam and neoprene rubber thermal tools, we are able to intensify the manipulation of energy, and also intensify the overall health benefits. By utilizing the ancient exercises along with the new modern tools, we have given birth to Dragonfly Qigong, Dragonfly Thermal Ball and Dragonfly Thermal Ruler.

The following two stories will introduce you to two of my top students, Sifu Patrick Albrecht, and (Sifu) Dr. James Barry M.D. They will tell you the stories behind their discoveries and contributions to Dragonfly Qigong exercises.

(SIFU) DR. JAMES BARRY'S STORY

"Mindful direction and walking with purposeful movements." This is a nice way to think of our lives, however in reality it is the serendipity or the awareness of the objects we trip or stumble over that brightens our existence and puts more energy in our steps.

I was working on a presentation for the local Alzheimer society for patients and their families, trying to explain the highly complex biochemical and anatomical changes in recognizable and understandable terms.

Alzheimer disease is a degenerative neurological condition

causing dementia. This is a particularly devastating disease because it robs the individual of his or her ability to use the mind, and it declines progressively over time. The loss of the mind diminishes the ability to use the energy of life and likewise restricts the ability of sharing our very nature with others.

The thought of energy and my need for meditation channeled me into a set of Taiji Ruler. (The use of a wooden device to increase the Qi flow when practicing Qigong and Taiji Quan)

When I returned to my task of preparing the presentation I picked up a piece of polyethylene foam (swimming pool flotation tube), which I had decided to use as a demonstration of normal tubular structure. This structure was a good representation of the microtubule cytoskeleton responsible for neuronal protein formation in the brain.

Protein formation-ENERGY- a microtubule at the cellular level that facilitates patterns of organic energy—WU LI.

I picked up the hollow tube and started to do the Taiji Ruler form. I remembered reading at one time that if a molecule of a substance was enlarged to the size of a baseball 14 stories high then an atom would be the size of a grape. Even in such a universally large space the vibration of air molecules would facilitate the increase of energy in the space it occupies. The response was quick and intense, much more so than with the wooden ruler or even using air alone. (Standing meditation or Wuji)

Why? There are many answers. From Traditional Chinese Medicine we can say we are experiencing a structure that is made up of two forms: solid, non-solid; hard, soft; wood, air; i.e. YIN and YANG.

Becoming aware of this concept has expanded my ability to experience Qigong and Taiji. Sharing this realization with Dr. Steward and watching him develop a program so that more students can awaken their abilities is a continual joy for me.

SIFU PATRICK ALBRECHT'S STORY

Our lives are complicated at times. We strive to make things easier and better at the same time. We even look to improve ancient Qigong exercises, which are already beneficial.

I was out shopping one day, looking for a lighter ball to use in our Tai-Qi ball exercises. My teacher, Dr. Steward, has several students in class who suffer from arthritis in their hands and wrists. The wooden ball is not that heavy normally, but to these students it was a burden. I found a five-inch, neoprene sport ball at the store, and decided to bring it to class and give it a try. Before I took it to class I decided to test it out during my own practice time at home.

What I discovered next was simply amazing. I began to do my exercises and my hands started to immediately increase their thermal temperature. I should have realized that this would have happened. I am a certified scuba diver and the balls were made out of the same material as my wet suit. The wet suit is a great thermal insulator for the diver's body. The neoprene suits keep the divers comfortable in the cool waters. Once the divers are out of the water the suits become extremely uncomfortable in the heat. While in the cool water they hold the coolness out, and hold the body's temperature in.

I proceeded to show this discovery to my teacher, Dr. Steward. He immediately discarded the old style wooden balls and adopted the thermal ball as a tool to use in all of the classes. The thermal ball acts like a mini generator of heat. I have been able to feel the Qi energy from the very first day. Using this new tool, along with Dr. Steward's Dragonfly exercises, I can definitely "feel" the energy moving between my palms. Performing the exercises with the new tools continually improves the effects of not only my Qigong, but my Tai-Qi practice as well. It is a great feeling knowing that I discovered an energy enhancement tool that everyone could use and benefit from.

IMAGERY AND VISUALIZATION

Imagery

"The Mind Leads The Body"

Imagery involves the use of imagination to create mental pictures - "images" - or situations. Imagery can help relieve pain, although the way it works is not completely understood. Imagery can be thought of as a daydream that requires all your senses - sight, touch, hearing, smell, and taste. Some people believe imagery is a form of self-hypnosis. Imagery can help people sleep, relax, relieve boredom, decrease anxiety and stress, and heal the body.

The first step in using imagery effectively then is relaxation. Relaxation has benefits besides preparing you for your Qigong imagery work. Regular deep relaxation can reduce blood pressure and enhance the immune system. This state can produce receptive imagery from the unconscious helping us to discover our needs and potential for problem solving.

Once your body is relaxed, your mind is calm and you are no longer thinking about that report due at work or school or what is for dinner, it is time to begin the imagery practice. In order to utilize imagery to the fullest you must first focus your attention on the skill you wish to enhance. Focus all of your attention on a clear and vivid image of yourself standing ready to begin your Qigong forms, and then focus on yourself performing each of the moves. If interfering thoughts or images enter your mind, take a deep breath and allow the image to pass by as you exhale. Then refocus on the Qigong image.

Imagery should not be confused with visualization. Imagery, in fact, does not require visualization at all to be effective. The objective in using imagery to enhance Qigong is not to see pretty pictures in your mind, but to pay attention, to be mindful, to train the body-mind. Imagery can utilize any or all of the senses. It certainly can include visual imagery, but may also include images of sounds, kinesthetic sensations, and even smells.

Imagery can be used to also enhance the over all effects of breathing while performing your forms. Imagine that while you are inhaling that coolness starts at the top of your head and proceeds to move down your back. As you exhale imagine that warmness moves up the front of your body to the top of your head. The whole cycle begins at the head and moves down to the sacrum and travels between the legs and then moves up the front of the body back to the head.

Imagery includes not only visual stimuli, but also other sensory modality. Feel the energy move freely through your body. Feel the heat of the energy accumulate in the areas that you desire. Incorporate as many senses as you can into your image. With practice, you will find that visualizing your image is easy, fun, and very relaxing.

Visualization

Visualization is an attention focusing technique of creating visual images in the mind. This is accomplished by harnessing the ingenuous power of our imagination for our own creation. We have all had some experience with visualization whether we are aware of it or not. We have all daydreamed about an upcoming exciting event during a mundane task such as a long drive or a household chore. We see what it's like in our mind's eye and feel the excitement, or we dread the upcoming meeting and our mind plays out the situation.

Since the mind reacts physiologically to imagined events the same way it does to real events, we can create health by imagining health, just as we can manifest anything else we desire in this way.

It is a well-known fact the chemical immune response of the body is affected both positively and negatively by stimuli. Consider the role that unreleased stress plays on our health. Likewise, visions of pleasure and peace can restore balance to the ravaged body, in addition to creating a feeling of relaxed calm. Visualization is simple to do. Form a clear picture in your mind of what you choose to manifest. If you are not able to actually "see" this in your mind's eye, that's okay. Just hold the idea in your thoughts. Focus on this image frequently throughout the day, everyday, giving it positive energy.

The alpha or hypnotic state amplifies the power of your imagery and your affirmations to produce your intended manifestation. If your images become real enough, they produce the same feelings and physical reactions as the actual objects or situations would if you were experiencing them in reality. Some visualization techniques do not utilize an altered state of consciousness, but I prefer to go into alpha when possible to deepen the visualization experience. Alpha state helps me to be more aware of my body so I feel the health benefits sooner and the effects seem to last longer. Determine what you desire in your world, be it health, inner calm, happiness, whatever, then enter into alpha state and visualize your world in that way. Use the power of your mind to create. Once becoming accustomed to visualization, many people find it very easy to slip back to these healing images whenever they allow themselves the space and the quiet time to do so. Utilizing the technique of visualization created a major shift in consciousness for me. Regular practice helped my body become stronger, less fatigued and less pained. This helped me to get in touch with the old me that used to be so strong, healthy, and fun loving.

There is no limit to what you can manifest with all the visualization possibilities. Whatever you can imagine, you can create. My favorite healing vision is one of me standing on a tropical beach. In a safe and protected area within this beautiful place, I am standing with my toes dug deep into the sand, I am at rest, and I sensually feel the warm sun penetrating into my body. The warming sun melting into my center, the glowing warmth spreading out into my chest and thighs, radiating out to the very tips of my toes and fingers, to the top of my head. Warm glowing sunshine moving all through my body, healing my body, healing every aching muscle, every stressed cell. The sun is gently warming my entire body and occasionally I feel the cool mist of the ocean spray upon my face

Another of my favorite visualizations is to imagine that every system of my body is working in perfect harmony. I become quiet and go into an alpha state where I focus on my body, particularly on my immune system, organs and cells. I see them powerfully active and happy, working to heal my body. When I used to feel cold all the time I would focus on an inner flame in my solar plexus warming my entire body and soul. When I am bored with the mundane, I often take from life by visualizing my favorite places in nature. My body actually feels like I am there and I feel the exhilaration of the wilderness in my soul. This visualization reconnects me to nature that fills me with the power I need to live my life fully. I often use visualization as an asset to my athletic training, as do many Olympic and professional athletes.

Visualization Techniques:

1. Visualize from your "minds eye" or as you would see it.

2. Visualize with as many of your senses as possible. Try to re-create as many feelings and muscular stimuli with each visualization as you can.

3. Visualize as many times during the day as possible, when you wake up, before training, after training and always before you fall asleep.

4. Visualize all the various situations that you will be facing.

5. Visualize those skills or plays which are the most difficult for you. It is important that the images are as perfect as possible, include as much of the physical feeling of doing these techniques as you can.

6. Repeat each image in your mind as many times as possible. Utilize every opportunity to reinforce neuromuscular patterning and energy manipulation.

Visualization is a controlled mode of thinking – applied, disciplined imagination. What we habitually visualize, is what we come to believe, and what we create in our lives.

Imagery and visualization are the main ingredients for success. Visualization with the use of imagery is thinking and seeing yourself perform positively and successfully in all situations: whether it is in the classroom, at training or in a competitive realm. Visualization and imagery development varies with each individual depending on his or her commitment to the process.

DRAGONFLY QIGONG EXERCISES

DRAGONFLY EXERCISES

The hands are windows into the entire practice of Qigong. The powers of giving and receiving, initiating contact and expression, so important in Qigong, are seen clearly in them. In this sense the hands act as extensions of the organism, magnifying and amplifying spiritual realities as a projected center.

When practicing the Dragonfly Qigong exercises, your sensations of Qi will be heightened. Sensations such as tingling, heat, slight sweating, or Qi movements along the specific pathways, may be felt. Most people will feel a warm or heat sensation. When you lead the Qi down, you may also feel the bottom of your feet, the Yongquan (bubbling well) Points, have a sensation of heat. These are all good sensations and are normal.

Dragonfly Qigong is capable of smoothing out the channels in the entire body. The goal is to have all the energy pathways flowing smoothly. Once this is accomplished, all illnesses can be eliminated. One can be trained while standing, sitting, or lying down.

Dragonfly Qigong involves moving the palms very slowly until some sensation is felt in your palms or/and fingers. With practice, the energy field feels larger as the sensations become stronger, and can be felt with the hands further apart. The purpose of the training is to stimulate the Qi circulation by setting up gentle, circular rhythms in the body. The practitioners hold either the thermal rod or the thermal ball between the palms, coordinating the movements of the hands and body, and connecting the energy flow with correct mechanics.

The training cultivates the three internal treasures, Essence, Qi and Spirit, while externally training the tendons, muscles, bones, and joints. All the movements are slow and gentle, with conservation of energy and use of core body mechanics as an underlying principle of training.

The exercises involve variations of rocking the body side-to-side, forward and backward while circling the Thermal Ruler or

Thermal Ball either vertically or horizontally in front of the body.

The hand movements and breathing during Dragonfly Qigong exercises are all circular in motion. As you push the hands outwards in the circle, you breathe out - yang. As the hands circle back and return to the body, you breathe in - yin.

The visualization of the circle as it journeys should include the dantian, spine, shoulders and head, and the breathing should be deep - you breathe in through the nose, and you exhale either through the nose or mouth.

Persistent practice for a few months or even a shorter period will produce effects to varying degrees, resulting in clear thinking, better memory, greater energy, broad-mindedness, fluent circulation of Qi and blood, enhanced appetite, better digestion and lighter footsteps.

Dragonfly Qigong can be used for self-healing or as a preparation for any form of energy work such as Taiji Quan, or as a pre-sport preparatory exercise. Dragonfly Qigong will enhance any Qigong form you are currently practicing, and it is a great introduction to the power of Qigong for those with no previous experience.

The Standard Qigong Principles

These rules or guidelines are generally observed unless specified otherwise.

- Breathe through the nose. (Unless specified to do otherwise)
- Tongue lightly touching the roof of the mouth (palate).
- Calm the mind.
- Hollowing the chest and rounding the back.
- Sense the body.
- Listen to the silence; see, taste, touch and smell the silence.
- Body relaxed, no physical tension.
- Shoulders soft.
- Relax the hips and keep the pelvis tucked.
- Imagine an invisible string pulling the crown of your head straight up.
- Gradually deepen the breathing.

- Breathe into the dantian. Expand the lower abdomen when inhaling, and contract the lower abdomen upon when exhaling. This is called lower diaphragmatic breathing.

Standing

Checklist of items for standing meditation:

- Feet shoulder width apart.
- Head and neck stacked on top of spine. (Like a stack of golden coins)
- Pelvis tipped up slightly.
- Knees slightly bent, enough that they are not straight or locked.
- Weight distributed evenly between the two feet.
- Weight distributed over the entire surface of each foot.
- The crown of the head lifts upward.
- Arms are held in a specified position according to the specific exercise being performed.
- Fingers are spaced, neutral and naturally curled.

Qi Pearl Exercise

1

2

3

4

Qi Pearl Exercise

This is a simple Qigong exercise that may allow you to begin to experience the effects of Qi flow.

With each exhalation imagine the Qi flowing down the Pericardium channel to the palm of the hand. Focus on the Laogong Point in the center of the palm. This is the Pericardium Point PC8. (Refer to Chapter 4) Begin to become aware of your experience at the Laogong Points on the two opposite palms as you continue to relax and breathe easily. You may have a variety of experiences- warmth, coolness, tingling, heaviness, a sense of attraction between the palms, and so on. Just be aware of the feeling.

Standing with your feet shoulder width apart with your knees slightly bent, hold your hands a comfortable distance in front of you, level with the middle of your torso. Your palms face each other approximately five to six inches apart. Your shoulders are relaxed.

1. Visualize a brilliant pearl of energy being held between your two hands. You imagine that the pearl is warm and comfortable to the touch.

2. Rotate the pearl so that your right hand comes on top and your left hand is beneath the pearl. Make sure that there is space under your armpits and around your elbows as you make this movement. Do not hunch your shoulders. All of the joints from your shoulders to your wrists and fingers should feel relaxed as you move.

3. Now rotate the pearl the other way, so that your left hand comes to the top and your right hand is under the pearl.

Play with the experience by bringing the two palms closer together and then pulling them apart. You may like to run the palm of one hand up the outside of the opposite arm from the thumb to the elbow. Keep it about an inch above the arm. Be aware if you experience any hot spots as you go, where Laogong seems to be making a connection with a point on the opposite arm. This may well be noticed at the point Hegu (on the fleshy mound between the thumb and the forefinger) or at the point Quchi, which is at the elbow.

Qigong Walking

This exercise was invented by the Chinese Government who gathered all of their leading Qigong experts to get together and design a simple form of Qigong that the whole population could learn easily and one that anyone at any age could perform. There is an acupuncture point at the base of the foot called the "bubbling well" point and it is the main or beginning kidney point in the body. This is where our Qi is said to 'spring' from in order to do work for us. If we activate this point then we activate the whole body. And this is what this exercise is all about. Some of the following exercises are stationary and some of the following exercises move utilizing the Qigong Walking methods. The exercises can be performed walking forwards, backwards or sideways.

We always pre-empt our Dragonfly Qigong exercises with head and face Qi washing, acupressure point massage activation, and Qi awakening exercises.

Head and Face Qi Washing Exercises

a. Preparation

- Sit or stand in a comfortable position and relax the whole body.
- Raise the tongue against the hard palate, have the eyes semi-closed. Remain in this position until the exercise is completed.
- Breathe slowly and evenly throughout the whole exercise.
- Focus the mind on the points of contact of your hands and fingers.

b. Push the forehead

- Rub with the index, middle and ring fingers of both hands.
- Start from the middle point between both eyebrows and push towards the center of the front hairline. Push evenly and steady for about one to two minutes and then repeat for a total of three repetitions.

c. Rub along the hairline

- With the same fingers, push up the center of the front hairline from the point in between the eyebrows.
- Rub along the hairline. The left hand moves towards the left and the right hand moves towards the right.
- Release pressure as the fingers reach the temples.
- Continue to rub for about one to two minutes.

d. Press the temples

- With the index or middle fingers, press and rub the temples in a circular manner.
- Move the fingers just above the ears to the back of the ears. Continue with the pressure as the fingers move.
- Press and rub the region in the back of the ear.
- Press for about one to two minutes.

e. Bath the face

- Place both palms on the center of the forehead and rub across it.
- Continue rubbing down both cheeks and upwards from the sides of the nose in a circular motion. Rub for about one or two minutes.

- Place both palms on the center of the forehead and rub down both sides of the nose, up the cheeks, the forehead and back to the center in a circular motion. Rub for about one or two minutes.

f. Comb the hair
- Keep the fingers slightly spread out and bent.
- Comb the hair with the fingers from the hairline down to the neck.
- Comb for about one to two minutes.

g. Brush the Gallbladder Channel
- With fingers on both sides of the head pointing towards the ears, brush the head from the tip of the ear, along its contour down to the base of the head.
- Brush for about one to two minutes.

h. Rub the back of the head
- With palms facing inwards, hands crossed and fingers interlocked, place both hands on the base of the head.
- Run both hands up and down the back of the head rhythmically.
- Do this for about one to two minutes.

After performing the Qi face washing techniques we massage the bubbling well point and the earth gate point on the bottom of each foot. These are the most powerful Points to treat the spirit and blood. These points balance yin; clear heat; subdue wind; calm the mind; restore consciousness; nourish the kidney; and suppress liver fire. They are the primary point to adjust and treat any vascular disturbance such as blood stagnation, blood pressure problems, or any other circulatory problem.

Massage these points several times on each foot to optimize their energy healing powers. These points are extremely tender on most people. Many health problems, both emotional and physical, can be resolved when treating these points due to its intimate connection to the blood.

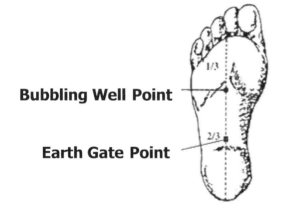

Bubbling Well Point

Earth Gate Point

Awakening the sleeping Dragon
"Qi Awakening Exercise"

The following Qi awakening exercise is my favorite. It is only one of many exercises that we utilized to awaken the "Sleeping Dragon". It is a very simple exercise that moves your Qi outward from the dantian all the way out to the distal aspects of your fingers.

While standing with your feet shoulder width apart, relax your shoulders and arms at your sides. With your knees slightly bent, your back straight, and your eyes looking straight ahead, swing both of your arms and hands loosely forwards until your hands are chest high. Now continue the motion by swing your arms and hands loosely backwards. Let the pendulum momentum of the swing carry them forward again. Slowly build up a smooth rapid swing, as if you were flinging your fingers outwards and immediately pulling them back quickly. You will begin to feel the Qi move into your palms and fingers. You will feel warmth and a tingling sensation. This is the "Awakening of the Sleeping Dragon". Begin with 30 to 50 complete swings.

Pre-empting Instructions for the Dragonfly Qigong Exercises

The following Dragonfly Qigong exercises can be performed with either the thermal ruler or the thermal ball. The exercises also can be stationary or they can move. To move with these exercises use a side stepping motion. When the thermal ruler or thermal ball moves towards the direction of your step slide the back leg towards the direction of movement, and when the thermal ruler or thermal ball comes back to its original starting position step out with the front leg. (Example: exercise is moving towards your right) Start with the thermal ruler or thermal ball on the left hip as you move the tool to the right hip in a circle; slide your left foot in towards the right foot. As the tool completes the circle and comes back to the left hip, slide your right foot out towards the right. Now repeat the movement until you have moved the desired distance down the floor. When you have moved the desired distance then simply reverse the stepping pattern and return to where you started. The breathing pattern should be as follows; always start with a deep inhale, and as you begin to move down the floor, exhale as your hands move in the direction of the stepping pattern.

"FLAT WHEEL" DRAGONFLY SOLO EXERCISE #1

A. Preparation Position

- Stand comfortably with your feet slightly wider than shoulder width.

- Place your palms on the ends of the thermal ruler or the sides of the thermal ball. Make sure that the hole in the end of the ruler is aligned with the Laogong Point in the palm of each hand.

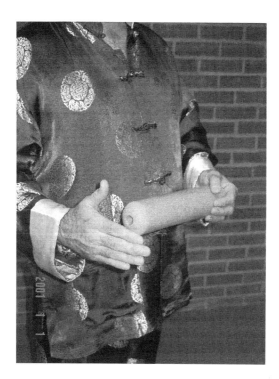

B. Breathing Method

- Inhale through the nose (mouth closed) and exhale through the nose.

- Expand the dantian while inhaling, and contract the dantian when exhaling.

- Inhale while the thermal ruler or thermal ball is moving towards your body and exhale when the thermal ruler or thermal ball is moving away from your body.

- The movements of your hands should replicate the slow deep diaphragmatic style of breathing. It is very important that you move your hands slowly and breathe slowly.

C. Flat Wheel Movement

1. While exhaling:

    - Shift your body weight forwards to the toes;

    - Move your hands and the thermal ruler or thermal ball away from your body as if you were stirring a large bowl.

    - Be careful to keep your hands and the thermal ruler or thermal ball in a plane, waist high, parallel to the ground.

2. While inhaling:

    - Shift your body weight backwards to the heels;

    - Move your hands and the thermal ruler or thermal ball towards your body as if you were stirring a large bowl.

    - Be careful to keep your hands and the thermal ruler or thermal ball in a plane, waist high, parallel to the ground.

Continue this exercise in the same direction for a total of thirty repetitions. Then change directions and complete the same exercise for a total of thirty repetitions.

"HIGH WHEEL" DRAGONFLY SOLO EXERCISE #2

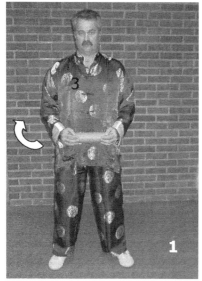

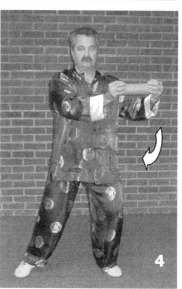

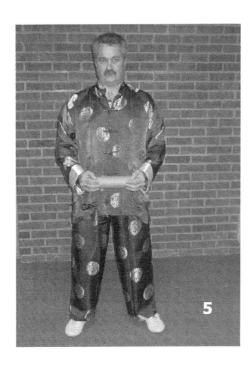

A. Preparation Position

- Stand comfortably with your feet slightly wider than shoulder width.

- Place your palms on the sides of the thermal ruler or thermal ball. Make sure that the hole in the end of the tube is aligned with the Laogong Point in the palm of each hand.

B. Breathing Method

- Inhale through the nose (mouth closed) and exhale through the nose.

- Expand the dantian while inhaling, and contract the dantian when exhaling.

- Inhale while the thermal ruler or thermal ball is moving upwards towards the sky, and exhale when the thermal ruler or thermal ball is moving downwards towards the ground. This movement is a large circle. Do not take the thermal ruler higher than the shoulders.

- The movements of your hands should replicate the slow deep diaphragmatic style of breathing. It is very important that you move your hands slowly and breathe slowly.

C. High Wheel Movement

1. While exhaling:

    - Shift your body weight from side to side, shifting the weight totally from leg to leg.

    - Exhale when the thermal ruler or thermal ball is moving downwards towards the ground. The hand movements are perpendicular to the floor. This movement is a large circle.

    - Be careful not to allow your hands and the thermal ruler or thermal ball to rise higher than the shoulders.

2. While inhaling:

    - Shift your body weight backwards to the heels.

- Inhale while the thermal ruler or thermal ball is moving upwards towards the sky. This movement is a large circle. Do not take the thermal ruler or thermal ball higher than the shoulders.

- Be careful not to allow your hands and the thermal ruler or thermal ball to rise higher than the shoulders.

Continue this exercise in the same direction for a total of thirty repetitions. Then change directions and complete the same exercise for a total of thirty repetitions.

"FIGURE EIGHT" DRAGONFLY SOLO EXERCISE #3

A. Preparation Position

- Stand comfortably with your feet slightly wider than shoulder width.

- Place your palms on the sides of the thermal ruler or thermal ball. Make sure that the hole in the end of the ruler is aligned with the Laogong Point in the palm of each hand.

B. Breathing Method

- Inhale through the nose (mouth closed) and exhale through the nose.

- Expand the dantian while inhaling, and contract the dantian when exhaling.

- Inhale while the thermal ruler or thermal ball is moving towards your body and exhale when the thermal ruler or thermal ball is moving away from your body.

- The movements of your hands should replicate the slow deep diaphragmatic style of breathing. It is very important that you move your hands slowly and breathe slowly.

C. Figure Eight Movement

1. While exhaling:

    - Shift your body weight forwards to the toes;

    - Move your hands and the thermal ruler or thermal ball away from your body as if you were tracing the number eight.

    - Be careful to keep your hands and the thermal ruler or thermal ball in a plane, waist high, parallel to the ground.

2. While inhaling:

    - Shift your body weight backwards to the heels;

    - Move your hands and the thermal ruler or thermal ball towards your body as if you were tracing the number eight.

    - Be careful to keep your hands and the thermal ruler or thermal ball level with your waist.

Continue this exercise in the same direction for a total of thirty repetitions. Then change directions and complete the same exercise for a total of thirty repetitions.

"DRAGONFLY THERMAL BALL OR THERMAL RULER" SOLO EXERCISE #4

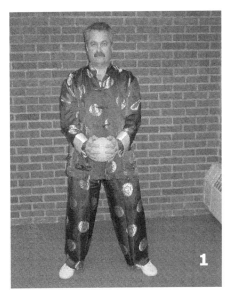
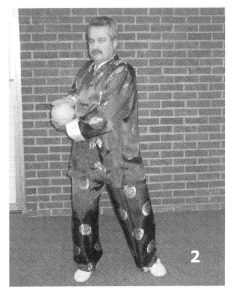
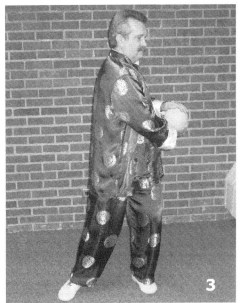

"DRAGONFLY THERMAL BALL OR THERMAL RULER" SOLO EXERCISE #4

A. Preparation Position

1. Stand comfortably with your feet slightly wider than shoulder width.

2. Place your palms on the sides of the thermal ruler or thermal ball. Make sure that the hole in the end of the ruler is aligned with the Laogong Point in the palm of each hand.

B. Breathing Method

1. Inhale through the nose (mouth closed) and exhale through the nose.

2. Expand the dantian while inhaling, and contract the dantian when exhaling.

3. Inhale while the thermal ruler or thermal ball is on your right hip, and exhale when the thermal ruler or thermal ball is on your left hip.

4. The movements of your hands should replicate the slow deep diaphragmatic style of breathing. It is very important that you move your hands slowly and breathe slowly.

C. Thermal Ball/Thermal Ruler Movement

- Shift your body weight towards to the right leg and place the thermal ruler or thermal ball on your right hip.

- Move your hands and the thermal ruler or thermal ball from your right hip toward the left hip and rotate the tool in front of your dantian (abdomen).

- Be careful to keep your hands and the thermal ruler or thermal ball in a plane, waist high, parallel to the ground.

- As the thermal tool moves towards the left hip, shift your body weight to the left leg and exhale.

Continue this exercise in the same direction for a total of thirty repetitions.

DRAGONFLY PARTNER EXERCISES

Sharing another person's energy is a wonderful component of Dragonfly Qigong. Utilizing a partners' energy along with your own only magnifies the end results. All my students find the partner exercises enjoyable and soothing.

The following Dragonfly Qigong exercises can be performed with either the thermal ruler or the thermal ball. The following exercises also can be stationary or they can move. One should always first practice these exercises in a stationary manner first prior utilizing them as moving exercises. To move with these exercises use a side stepping motion. When the thermal ruler or thermal ball moves towards the direction of your step slide the back leg towards the direction of movement, and when the thermal ruler or thermal ball comes back to its original starting position step out with the front leg. Now repeat the movement until you have moved the desired distance down the floor. When you have moved the desired distance then simply reverse the stepping pattern and return to where you started.

The breathing pattern should be as follows: always start with a deep inhale, and as you begin to move down the floor exhale as your hands move in the direction of the stepping pattern.

"DRAGONFLY CRICKET IN THE BOX"

THERMAL BALL-PARTNER EXERCISE #1

A. Preparation Position

- Stand comfortably with your feet slightly wider than shoulder width facing your partner.

- Place your palms on the sides of the thermal ball and place your partner's hand on the top and bottom of the thermal ball.

B. Breathing Method

- Inhale through the nose (mouth closed) and exhale through the nose.

- Expand the dantian while inhaling, and contract the dantian when exhaling.

- Inhale while the thermal ball is moving towards your body and exhale when the thermal ball is moving away from your body.

- The movements of your hands should replicate the slow deep diaphragmatic style of breathing. It is very important that you move your hands slowly and breathe slowly.

C. Cricket in the Box Movement

1. While exhaling:

    - Shift your body weight forwards to the toes.

- Move your hands and the thermal ball away from your body as if you were stirring a large bowl.

- Be careful to keep your hands and the thermal ball level with your waist.

2. While inhaling:

   a. Shift your body weight backwards to the heels.

   b. Move your hands and the thermal ball towards your body as if you were stirring a large bowl. Hand movements are performed parallel to the floor.

   c. Be careful to keep your hands and the thermal ball level with your waist.

Continue this exercise in the same direction for a total of thirty repetitions. Then change directions, also change hand positioning and direction of the thermal ball, and complete the same exercise for a total of thirty repetitions.

"FLAT WHEEL"

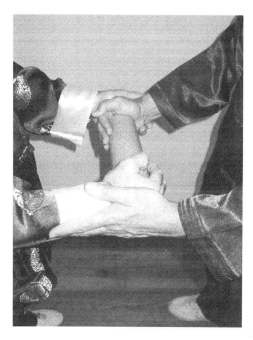

"FLAT WHEEL"

DRAGONFLY PARTNER EXERCISE #2

A. Preparation Position

- Stand comfortably with your feet slightly wider than shoulder width facing your partner.

- Each of you must place your right palms on one end of the thermal ruler or thermal ball. Make sure that the hole in the end of the ruler is aligned with the Laogong Point in the palm of each hand. Then cover your partner's right hand with your left hand. Be careful to place your palms so that the Laogong Point aligns itself with your partners Laogong Points.

B. Breathing Method

- Inhale through the nose (mouth closed) and exhale through the nose.

- Expand the dantian while inhaling, and contract the dantian when exhaling.

- Inhale while the thermal ruler or thermal ball is moving towards your body and exhale when the thermal ruler or thermal ball is moving away from your body.

- The movements of your hands should replicate the slow deep diaphragmatic style of breathing. It is very important that you move your hands slowly and breathe slowly.

C. Flat Wheel Movement

1. While exhaling:

    - Shift your body weight forwards to the toes;

    - Move your hands and the thermal ruler or thermal ball away from your body as if you were stirring a large bowl. Hand movements are performed parallel to the floor.

- Be careful to keep your hands and the thermal ruler or thermal ball level with your waist.

2. While inhaling:

　　d. Shift your body weight backwards to the heels.

　　e. Move your hands and the thermal ruler or thermal ball towards your body as if you were stirring a large bowl.

　　f. Be careful to keep your hands and the thermal ruler or thermal ball level with your waist.

Continue this exercise in the same direction for a total of thirty repetitions. Then change directions, also change hand positioning and direction of the thermal ruler or thermal ball, and complete the same exercise for a total of thirty repetitions.

"HIGH WHEEL"

"HIGH WHEEL"

DRAGONFLY PARTNER EXERCISE #3

A. Preparation Position

- Stand comfortably with your feet slightly wider than shoulder width facing your partner.

- Each of you must place your right palms on one end of the thermal ruler or thermal ball. Make sure that the hole in the end of the ruler is aligned with the Laogong Point in the palm of each hand. Then cover your partner's right hand with your left hand. Be careful to place your palms so that the Laogong Point aligns itself with your partners Laogong Points.

B. Breathing Method

- Inhale through the nose (mouth closed) and exhale through the nose.

- Expand the dantian while inhaling, and contract the dantian when exhaling.

- Inhale while the thermal ruler or thermal ball is moving towards your body and exhale when the thermal ruler or thermal ball is moving away from your body.

- The movements of your hands should replicate the slow deep diaphragmatic style of breathing. It is very important that you move your hands slowly and breathe slowly.

C. High Wheel Movement

1. While exhaling:

    - Shift your body weight from side to side, shifting the weight totally from leg to leg.

- Exhale when the thermal ruler or thermal ball is moving downwards towards the ground. The hand movements are perpendicular to the floor. This movement is a large circle. Do not take the thermal ruler higher than the shoulders.

- Be careful not to allow your hands and the thermal ruler or thermal ball to rise higher than the shoulders.

2. While inhaling:

    - Shift your body weight backwards to the heels.

    - Inhale while the thermal ruler or thermal ball is moving upwards towards the sky. The hand movements are perpendicular to the floor. This movement is a large circle. Do not take the thermal ruler or thermal ball higher than the shoulders.

    - Be careful not to allow your hands and the thermal ruler or thermal ball to rise higher than the shoulders

Continue this exercise in the same direction for a total of thirty repetitions. Then change directions, also change hand positioning and direction of the thermal ruler or thermal ball, and complete the same exercise for a total of thirty repetitions.

"FIGURE EIGHT" DRAGONFLY
PARTNER EXERCISE #4

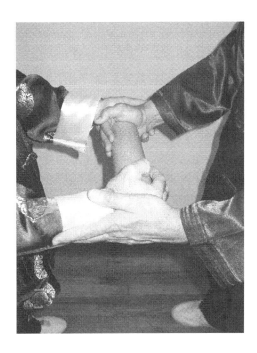

A. Preparation Position

- Stand comfortably with your feet slightly wider than shoulder width facing your partner.

- Each of you must place your right palms on one end of the thermal ruler or thermal ball. Make sure that the hole in the end of the ruler is aligned with the Laogong Point in the palm of each hand. Then cover your partner's right hand with your left hand. Be careful to place your palms so that the Laogong Point aligns itself with your partners Laogong Points.

B. Breathing Method

- Inhale through the nose (mouth closed) and exhale through the nose.

- Expand the dantian while inhaling, and contract the dantian when exhaling.

- Inhale while the thermal ruler or thermal ball is moving towards your body and exhale when the thermal ruler or thermal ball is moving away from your body.

- The movements of your hands should replicate the slow deep diaphragmatic style of breathing. It is very important that you move your hands slowly and breathe slowly.

C. Figure Eight Movement

1. While exhaling:

    - Shift your body weight forwards to the toes;

    - Move your hands and the thermal ruler or thermal ball away from your body as if you were tracing the number eight.

    - Be careful to keep your hands and the thermal ruler or thermal ball in a plane, waist high, parallel to the ground.

2. While inhaling:

    - Shift your body weight backwards to the heels.

    - Move your hands and the thermal ruler or thermal ball towards your body as if you were tracing the number eight.

    - Be careful to keep your hands and the thermal ruler or thermal ball in a plane, waist high, parallel to the ground.

Continue this exercise in the same direction for a total of thirty repetitions. Then change directions, also change hand positioning and direction of the thermal ruler or thermal ball, and complete the same exercise for a total of thirty repetitions.

"THE TIDE"

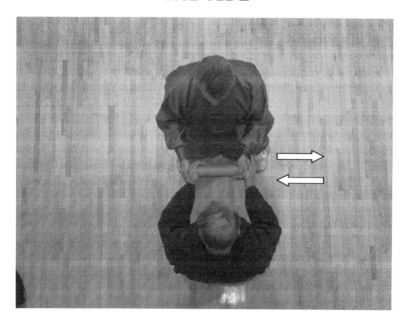

"THE TIDE"

DRAGONFLY PARTNER EXERCISE #5

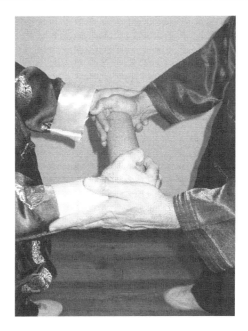

A. Preparation Position

- Stand comfortably with your feet slightly wider than shoulder width facing your partner.

- Each of you must place your right palms on one end of the thermal ruler or thermal ball. Make sure that the hole in the end of the ruler is aligned with the Laogong Point in the palm of each hand. Then cover your partner's right hand with your left hand. Be careful to place your palms so that the Laogong Point aligns itself with your partners Laogong Points.

B. Breathing Method

- Inhale through the nose (mouth closed) and exhale through the nose.

- Expand the dantian while inhaling, and contract the dantian when exhaling.

- Always exhale when moving the thermal ruler and thermal ball towards the direction you are stepping towards.

- The movements of your hands should replicate the slow deep diaphragmatic style of breathing. It is very important that you move your hands slowly and breathe slowly.

C. The Tide Movement

- Shift your body weight from side to side, shifting the weight totally from leg to leg.

- Exhale when the thermal ruler or thermal ball is moving towards the direction you will be moving. This movement is a horizontal movement that is parallel to the floor and moves side to side.

- Be careful to keep your hands and the thermal

ruler or thermal ball in a plane, waist high, parallel to the ground.

Continue this exercise in the same direction for a total of thirty repetitions. Then change directions, also change hand positioning and direction of the thermal ruler or thermal ball, and complete the same exercise for a total of thirty repetitions.

"FLAT WHEEL HANDSHAKE"

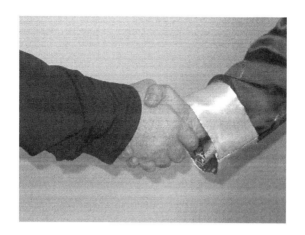

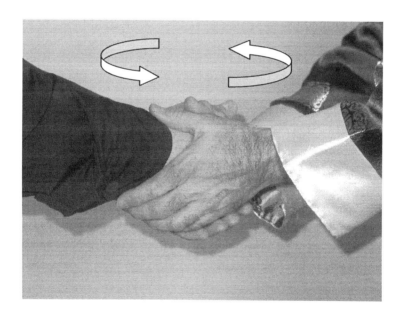

"FLAT WHEEL HANDSHAKE"
DRAGONFLY PARTNER EXERCISE #6

A. Preparation Position

- Stand comfortably with your feet slightly wider than shoulder width facing your partner.

- Each of you must place your right hands together, as if you are shaking hands. Then cover your partner's right hand with your left hand. Be careful to place your palms so that the Laogong Point aligns itself with your partners Laogong Points.

B. Breathing Method

- Inhale through the nose (mouth closed) and exhale through the nose.

- Expand the dantian while inhaling, and contract the dantian when exhaling.

- Inhale while your hands are moving towards your body and exhale when your hands are moving away from your body.

- The movements of your hands should replicate the slow deep diaphragmatic style of breathing. It is very important that you move your hands slowly and breathe slowly.

C. Flat Wheel Movement

1. While exhaling:

    - Shift your body weight forwards to the toes;

    - Move your hands away from your body as if you were stirring a large bowl.

    - Be careful to keep your hands in a plane, waist high, parallel to the ground.

2. While inhaling:

    - Shift your body weight backwards to the heels.

    - Move your hands towards your body as if you were stirring a large bowl.

    - Be careful to keep your hands in a plane, waist high, parallel to the ground.

Continue this exercise in the same direction for a total of thirty repetitions. Then change directions, also change hand positioning and complete the same exercise for a total of thirty repetitions.

As you do these simple exercises you will begin to experience the effect of Qi flow, whether as heat, tingling feelings, or whatever. Remember, the sensation is not the Qi; it is the effect of Qi.

Think of this analogy. If electricity passes through a wire it will meet resistance. If the resistance rises, the current flow will cause the wire to heat up. The heat in the wire is not the electricity, it is the effect of the electrical flow.

Dragonfly Qigong allows you to experience this exercise in the same way. What you are experiencing is the effect of Qi. The point I would like to emphasize is that there is no one sensation to be looking for. The sensations experienced can vary, but some form of warmth tends to be the most common. If you practice Qigong exercises on a regular basis then your ability to become aware of your own Qi flow, and indeed of that of other people, will develop markedly.

DRAGONFLY THERMAL RULER EXERCISES

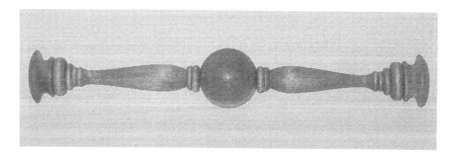

Figure 6-Old Style Wooden Golden Ruler (Chih-Ruler)

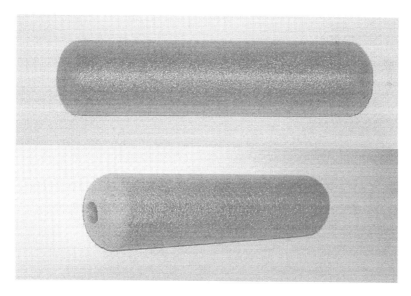

Figure 7-New Style Closed Cell Hollow Core Foam Thermal Ruler

The Dragonfly Thermal Ruler also called the Taiji Golden Ruler is a unique form of Qigong. It is a system of Taoist Yoga, or energy exercises, which employs a special tool called the Thermal Ruler. The Dragonfly Thermal Ruler has seven "internal" basic exercises and eight advanced exercises. The exercises are performed in repetition with the Thermal Ruler held between the palms on a meridian Point called the pericardium point or Laogong Point. The exercises specially coordinate movement, breath, mental focus, and visual focus along the energy meridians of the body, cultivating the body's energy or Qi. The Dragonfly Thermal Ruler aligns and empowers major energy reservoirs, or "dantians", and energy meridians of the body.

This Chinese energy philosophy somewhat parallels the human sympathetic nervous and cerebral-spinal systems. The human body has three dantian energy reservoirs. The lower dantian is located one to two inches below the navel. The second is located in the chest area close to the sternum, and the third dantian is located in the head area. The practitioner must always take care in aligning his/her movements with these energy centers. Constant practice of these exercises imparts good health and longevity by cultivating Qi, and balancing it throughout the body.

The Taiji Ruler is typically made of light porous wood and comes in many shapes, depending on which Taiji Ruler system is being practiced. Like all martial arts there are several different versions of the Taiji Ruler exercises existing today.

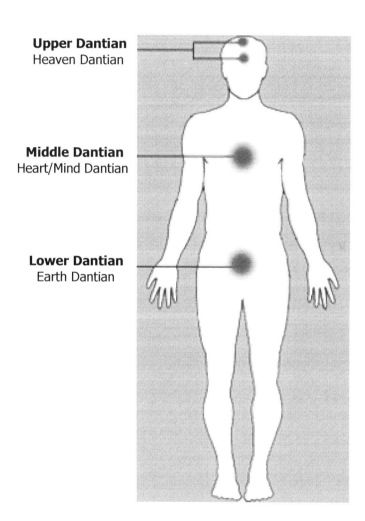

Three Dantians or Three Treasures

For many years we have used and depended on the ancient tools of Taiji Ball and Taiji Ruler. These tools were either made of porous lightweight wood or steel. Thanks to a couple of my ingenious students we have utilized new modern materials that expedite the healing benefits of these ancient exercises. Persistent practice for a few months or even a shorter period will produce effects to varying degrees, resulting in clear thinking, better memory, greater energy, broad-mindedness, fluent circulation of Qi and blood, enhanced appetite, better digestion and lighter footsteps.

Sometime during the Sung Dynasty the Golden Ruler exercises were born. The true story of the ruler's inception, like so many other oriental things, is shrouded in mists of legend and folklore. Legend however holds that the Taiji Golden Ruler was invented by a famous Taoist, Chen Hsi-I. Chen Hsi-I was a friend and retainer to the first emperor of the Sung Dynasty, and taught many styles of martial arts to the royal family. The Taiji Ruler was then transmitted down through the ages and disseminated by the

Sung emperor's descendents. Although the Taiji Ruler and Taiji Quan share a similar theme, they have different origins and histories of transmission. Due to the widespread exchange and crossover between various martial arts, several Taiji masters also teach the exercises of the Taiji Ruler.

The daily practice of the Thermal Ruler exercises promotes health and strength. Like Taiji Quan, the Dragonfly Thermal Ruler develops balance, harmony and integration in all human processes. The Dragonfly Thermal Ruler exercises accomplish this by working through the central nervous system and thereby effectively exercising the entire physiology, not just a few muscle groups and the cardiovascular system. Some of the immediate benefits are improved posture, circulation, metabolism, neuromuscular functioning, and the strengthening of the immune system.

There are several health benefits to the Dragonfly Thermal Ruler, and these can be easily accessible by practicing the following principles:

1. The body is in a state of complete relaxation.
2. All movements are circular and spiraling.

3. All movement is controlled by the turning of the waist.

4. The spine is held straight and erect.

5. The eyes are constantly focused on the Thermal Ruler.

6. Breathing is coordinated with all movements.

7. Breathing occurs at a rate of two breaths per minute.

8. Breathing in through the nose, and exhaling out the mouth.

Each exercise focuses, channels, balances and distributes Qi along specific pathways and energy centers. This cultivation begins with exercise #1, encouraging Qi movement along a "grand circulation"-moving up the back and down the anterior body, which follows a path extending from head to toe-on both lateral sides of the body. Then this grand circulation of Qi is concentrated on one side of the body and then the other by exercise #2. With exercise #3, the focus of Qi mobilization is placed on the pathway from the waist through the torso and the arms. Exercise #4 emphasizes generation of Qi through the internal organs, through vigorous work of the legs. Then exercise #5 shifts the focus of Qi cultivation to the energy center of the body. Then with exercise #6, Qi movement is activated from head to toe again, but in a reverse circulation of exercise #1. Finally, the Qi of the highest energy center is balanced by exercise #7.

BASIC STANCES

FRONT STANCE/BOW STANCE

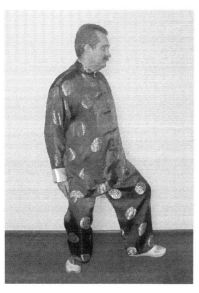 

SITTING/BACK STANCE   **HORSE STANCE**

SEVEN BASIC EXERCISES

BASIC EXERCISE #1

The first exercise of the Dragonfly Thermal Ruler consists of four 45 degree angle steps forward, beginning with the left foot, followed by a 180 degree turn-about, and then four steps back to the starting Point, and the a 180 degree turn-about and a cleansing breath rotation of the Thermal Ruler.

1. To begin, hold the Thermal Ruler in front of the body with arms naturally hanging and extended by gravity. Sink your weight into the right leg, bending the knee, and step 45 degrees to the left, with your left foot, leading with the toes, and sliding the sole of your foot along the floor or ground surface. As you sink into the right leg, slowly raise the Thermal Ruler to the level of the heart and, as you shift forward to the left leg, roll the Thermal Ruler outward to eye level and then downward with gravity, following a circular path and fully extending the arms.

2. As your weight comes forward over the left leg, slowly raise the Thermal Ruler in front of your body, bending the elbows and pulling the right leg in alongside the now-weighted left leg.

3. When all your weight has shifted to the left leg, turn your torso 90 degrees to the right, keeping the left foot in place, and slide the right foot forward towards the right corner at a 45 degree angle, skimming the floor with the sole. As you pivot to this right corner, you are simultaneously raising the Thermal Ruler from its lowest position to about solar plexus level. Continue the circular movement by shifting forward, bringing the right knee over the right toes, and circle the Thermal Ruler from chest level upward and outward to eye level, extending the arms. Allow the Thermal Ruler to continue moving on a downward arc with the arms extended, as your weight shifts fully forward over the right foot.

4. Now, same as we did on the left leg continue circling the Thermal Ruler into the body (arms fully extended downward) and raise the Thermal Ruler along the front of the body, while

simultaneously drawing in the left leg alongside the right. Imagine that there is a string attaching the Thermal Ruler to your left foot, so that the foot comes in as the Thermal Ruler rises and "pulls" it in. All your body weight should be supported by the right leg.

5. Once the left leg comes in to the right, keep the right foot in place (Pointing 45 degrees right) and turn the torso 90 degrees to the left. Slide the left foot forward with the sole skimming the floor and shift forward to do another roll of the Thermal Ruler.

    This is the third repetition.

6. After completing the third repetition, you are facing 45 degrees to the left corner. Next, step to the right 45 degrees to the right corner. Slide the right foot forward and roll the Thermal Ruler forward and up to eye level. As the Thermal Ruler moves along its downward arc and comes into the body, turn the entire body to the left 180 degrees, pivoting on the ball of the right foot, and assume a sitting stance (the weight is 80% on the back leg) facing the direction from which you came. Shift your weight

forward to the left leg as you roll out the Thermal Ruler once more 45 degrees to the left corner.

7. Continue with three more repetitions of this stepping/shifting movement.

8. The fourth and last repetition faces the starting Point and is done with the right foot forward. To end this cycle, as the Thermal Ruler moves along its downward arc and comes into the body, turn the entire body to the left 180 degrees, pivoting on the ball of the right foot, and assume a sitting stance facing the direction from which you came. Then raise the Thermal Ruler to eye level while drawing in the left foot alongside the right. Settle your weight equally on both feet, straighten both legs and simultaneously lower the Thermal Ruler from eye level to the hips. This last cycle ends with an exhalation. You should be standing on the exact position on which you began, and you should be facing the same direction as you did in the beginning.

1

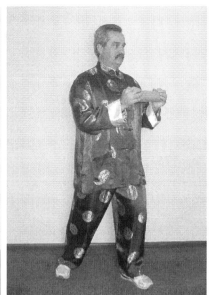

2

3

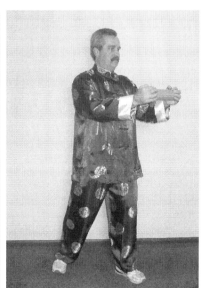

4

5

6

BASIC EXERCISE #2

The second exercise is done with the feet stationary in two postures. Eight repetitions are done in the first position and then another eight in the second position.

1. Stand comfortably erect with your feet together, arms down holding the Thermal Ruler in front of the body. Bend both knees; sink your weight into the right leg and step to the left 45 degrees with the left foot so that you have a Thermal Ruler's distance between your two heels.

2. Now shift your weight forward, moving from the lower dantian, and roll the Thermal Ruler upward and outward to eye level. When your left knee is over the toes, your arms are extended-but not rigid or locked at the elbows. Then slowly shift back to the right leg keeping the left foot in place and lower the Thermal Ruler with gravity along an inward-circling path. When your weight has fully

shifted back to the right leg, the Thermal Ruler has come in towards the body at dantian level.

3. Continue the movement by shifting forward again, bringing the Thermal Ruler upwards towards heart level. Observe all the principles of Taiji: relax the entire body and sink the posture, shift your weight clearly. Keep the back straight, and allow the movement to flow like water from the ground upward through the legs, the waist, up the torso, and finally expressed through shoulder, elbow, wrist and fingertips.

4. Each roll or circling of the Thermal Ruler starting from the lower dantian level and returning back to the lower dantian, is counted as one repetition. Slowly and comfortably do eight repetitions with the left foot forward.

5. After completing the eighth roll, simultaneously shift your weight fully onto the left leg, raise the Thermal Ruler to eye level and bring in the right foot alongside the left, keeping both knees bent. Keep the left foot in place and

pivot the torso 90 degrees to the right, so that you are facing the right corner. Slowly extend the right foot forward, getting the Thermal Ruler's distance between the heels.

6. Proceed with eight repetitions on the right foot. The movement is centered in the dantian, driven by the legs, and led by the back, which pulls the arms in with Thermal Ruler in hands.

7. After the eighth repetition is completed, shift all of your weight forward to the right leg and simultaneously raise the Thermal Ruler to eye level and bring the left foot in alongside the right, keeping both knees bent. Now exhale and simultaneously lower the Thermal Ruler and stand up, straightening both legs.

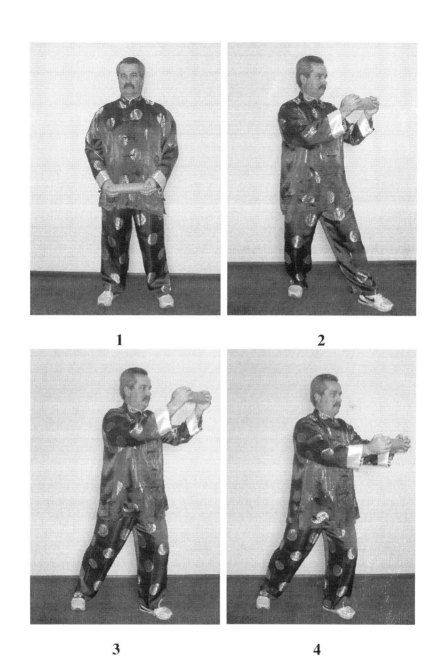

5 **6**

BASIC EXERCISE #3

The third exercise is done with the feet stationary in two postures. Eight repetitions are done in the first position and then another eight in the second position.

1. Stand with legs straight holding the Thermal Ruler at dantian level. Pivot the torso 45 degrees to the left and slide-step the left foot out while supporting all of your weight on the right leg.

2. Raise the Thermal Ruler upward in front of the body and then move it outward away from the body while simultaneously shifting the hips backward and straightening the left leg, and lowering the back forward and downward towards the horizontal. Continuing sitting back onto the right leg (which is bent) and completely stretch the torso and arms downward along the length of the left leg. Make sure the left foot remains flat on the floor. This completes half the cycle.

3. The second half of the cycle is done as follows: Slowly raise the torso and allow the arms to just hang relaxed from the shoulders. By doing so, you will notice the Thermal Ruler moving up from your foot, and over your shin, as you raise your back. As the Thermal Ruler passes above the left knee, shift your weight forward and move the left knee to come forward over the toes. As you shift forward, the back continues to rise to the vertical, and the Thermal Ruler is raised to chest level. This movement from the torso-lowered-on-the left-leg position, to the vertical right bow stance (80% of the body weight is on the front leg) posture is coordinated with the inhalation.

4. From this upright position with left knee over the toes, simultaneously execute the following movements:

   a. bend in the hips

   b. lower the torso towards horizontal

    c.   extend the arms holding the Thermal Ruler outwards towards horizontal

    d.   shift weight back to the right leg

Continue lowering the torso with arms outstretched bringing the Thermal Ruler all the way down to the floor beyond the left foot if possible. This portion of the cycle, from the push posture to the "torso-lowered-on-leg" position, is coordinated with exhalation.

5. Complete the cycle by simultaneously raising the torso, shifting forward to the left bow stance (left knee over toes) and raising the Thermal Ruler to chest level.

6. Do eight repetitions with the left foot forward, moving as slowly as possible, while maintaining comfortable coordination of each part of the movement, with inhalation and exhalation.

7. After the eighth repetition, shift forward, close the rear

foot into the front foot, and bring the Thermal Ruler up to eye level, as we did to end exercises one and two.

Keeping both knees bent and the left foot in place, pivot the torso 90 degrees to the right and slide-step the right foot forward. Now proceed with eight slow repetitions of the exact same movements with the right foot forward.

The finish is the same as exercises one and two.

1   **2**

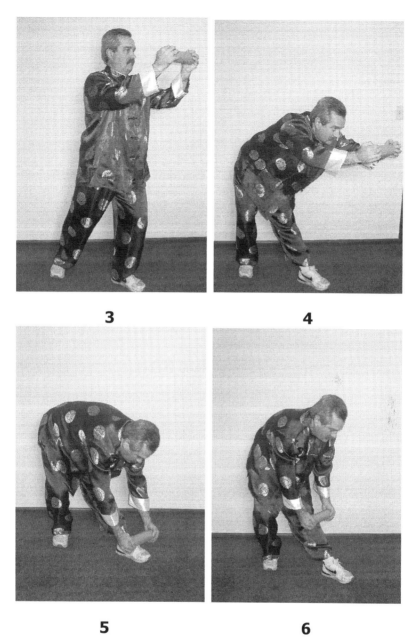

3

4

5

6

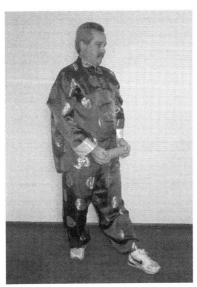 

7 **8**

BASIC EXERCISE #4

Exercise four moves the body down and then up, repeatedly building great strength in the legs, and the entire body. With each downward movement the Thermal Ruler circles downward at a comfortable arms' length away from the body, and then with each upward movement the Thermal Ruler moves upward staying very close to the body.

1. Begin by stepping 45 degrees to the left and getting a Thermal Ruler's distance between the heels. Inhale slowly and shift the weight forward so that the left knee comes over the toes, and raise the Thermal Ruler to eye level.

2. Next exhale, bend both knees and slowly lower the entire posture all the way down to a squatting position and simultaneously roll the Thermal Ruler outward and lower it down through your field of vision, to the level of your front knee and the dantian. Keep your back straight and upright as you lower your posture. As you sink

downward, allow the heel of the rear foot to come up off the ground while keeping your front foot flat. Your weight subtly shifts from 100% on the rear leg while in the standing position to 60% on the front leg at the lowest kneeling position. At the lowest position in this exercise, your buttocks are barely touching, but not resting on the heel of the rear (right) foot. Coordinate the entire sinking action with one exhalation through the mouth.

3. Once you have reached the lowered position and have reached the limit of your exhalation and abdominal contraction, slowly inhale and straighten the legs, raising the posture back towards the standing position. As you start to rise, do not take quick, uncontrolled gulps of air. Keep the back vertical as you rise. Do not lean forward, as that is the most common error. Coordinate the entire standing action with one inhalation. Move as slowly as possible without losing control of your breath. Keep your eyes focused on the Thermal Ruler and hands. As you rise to the standing position, your weight shifts fully back to

the rear (right) and the Thermal Ruler is brought to the upper chest and throat level. This completes one cycle on the left side.

4. Now begin a second cycle by slowly shifting forward and rolling the Thermal Ruler outward and up to eye level. Then begin to exhale, bend the knees, and sink downward again. Complete this second cycle by rising slowly with the inhalation.

5. For each subsequent repetition, remember to exhale on the sinking-squatting action, and inhale-imagine inflating and lifting yourself with each rising-standing action. Anchor your mind in the dantian region (lower belly), and imagine that the expansion and contraction of Qi in the dantian is what lifts and lowers your movement. Keep the back vertical throughout the exercise.

6. Beginners should try to do the sinking action with an exhalation of no less than four seconds, and come up to the standing position, with an inhalation of four seconds.

Do not strain in any way in attempting to extend the time of your breaths and movements.

After several months of daily practice without strain, you will find that your breath capacity has naturally expanded; so that you can do each exercise with inhales and exhales of ten seconds, or more. It is the expansion of both ends of the breath cycle that qualifies the Dragonfly Thermal Ruler as an art of Qigong.

7. After completing eight repetitions on the left leg, proceed to the right leg and repeat the exercise eight more repetitions.

1

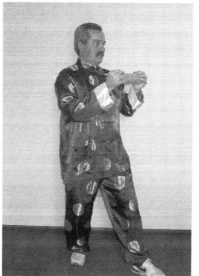

2

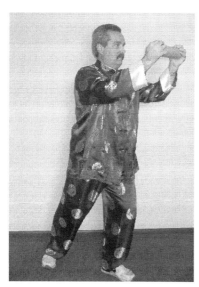

3

4

5

BASIC EXERCISE #5

Exercise five is performed in a traditional horse stance as demonstrated in the exercise photos. The stance requires the feet to be placed approximately two shoulder widths apart.

1. With the feet properly placed, inhale and raise the Thermal Ruler to eye level. Sink the torso down by bending the knees, and lower the Thermal Ruler to the lower dantian level. Keep your back straight and your head level. Keep both knees bowed out over the ankles.

2. Holding the Thermal Ruler horizontally to start, exhale, turn your waist and carry the Thermal Ruler to the left side of the body, at hip level. Slowly inhale and turn the Thermal Ruler to the vertical, rolling the left palm over the right palm. Take as long and as deep an inhalation as you comfortably can. Then slowly exhale, turn the waist to the right, and carry the Thermal Ruler (with the left palm over the right palm) through a 180-degree arc to the right side of the body. Keep the Thermal Ruler vertical and at hip

level. As you carry the Thermal Ruler from the left side to the right side, exhale slowly and evenly.

3. Once the Thermal Ruler is on the right side of the body, slowly inhale and rotate the Thermal Ruler so that the right palm comes over the left palm. Then slowly exhale and smoothly carry the Thermal Ruler across the front of the body to the left side again. The Thermal Ruler is held vertically at hip level. This completes one repetition of this exercise.

4. For starters, try to take five seconds on each inhalation and five seconds for each exhalation. No matter how much time you take to breathe, it is important that the duration of each inhalation is the same as the duration of each exhalation.

5. Do a total of eight repetitions. After completing the eighth and last pass, bring the Thermal Ruler to the center position in front of the lower dantian. Then slowly straighten the legs, standing up from the horse stance, raising the Thermal Ruler to eye level. When both legs are straightened, exhale through the mouth and lower the Thermal Ruler from eye level, back down to the dantian level.

1

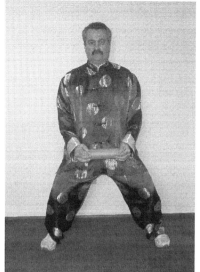

2

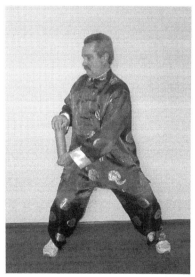

3

4

5

6

7

BASIC EXERCISE #6

Exercise six is identical to exercise number one, with the exception of the Thermal Ruler's grand rotation. The Thermal Ruler's rotation is the exact opposite of exercises one, two, three and four. With each step, the Thermal Ruler circles so that the upper arc curves inward toward the upper body and the lower arc rolls outward in the same direction as the slide-step.

1

2

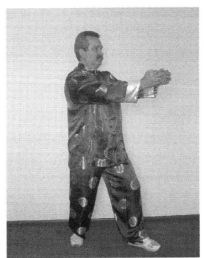
3

4

5

BASIC EXERCISE #7

Exercise seven is performed in the seated position. Seat yourself on a stool or a table high enough that your feet hang above the floor. Keep your legs together, but not tense. Hold the Thermal Ruler in your palms, resting it in your lap.

1. Inhale slowly and simultaneously raise the Thermal Ruler to eye level keeping it horizontal and angle your feet upward, toes pointing towards the ceiling. Keep your toes in this raised position for the entire exercise.

2. Gently exhale and carry the Thermal Ruler to your left, just outside your temple, keeping it horizontal and gazing at the Thermal Ruler's center. Follow the Thermal Ruler with your eyes, but do not turn the head more than a few degrees.

3. Slowly inhale and turn the Thermal Ruler so that your left palm goes above your right. Keep the Thermal Ruler at eye level.

4. When the Thermal Ruler reaches the vertical, slowly exhale and move the Thermal Ruler to the right in a 180-degree arc to just outside your right temple. Keep your eyes continually focused on the center of the Thermal Ruler.

5. When you have carried the Thermal Ruler to your right side, inhale slowly and turn the Thermal Ruler counter-clockwise so that the right palm comes over the left palm.

6. Now bring the Thermal Ruler across to the left side, again on the exhalation, counting this as one repetition.

7. To complete this exercise you must perform eight repetitions. After the eighth repetition, with the Thermal Ruler on the left side of the head, with the left palm over the right palm, rotate the Thermal Ruler 90 degrees clockwise, so that it comes back to horizontal. Immediately, but slowly, bring the Thermal Ruler directly in front of your eyes. All of this is done with one deep inhalation.

8. Then exhale and simultaneously lower the Thermal Ruler to your lap and release your upward-Pointed toes to their natural position.

1   2

2   4

5

6

EIGHT ADVANCED EXERCISES

Each exercise in the advanced exercises orbits the Thermal Ruler between a point on the lower body and the lower dantian, the middle dantian and the upper dantian. (See diagram on page 124) The lower dantian (Earth Dantian) is located two inches below the navel. The middle dantian (Heart/Mind Dantian) is at the level of the solar plexus. The upper dantian (Heaven Dantian) is located in the area between the center of the eyebrows and the top of the skull. The practitioner must carefully align his/her movements of the Thermal Ruler with the indicated dantian (energy reservoir).

ADVANCED EXERCISE #1

1. Start with both feet parallel, pointing forward with a Thermal Ruler's distance between the heels. Turn both feet 45 degrees to the left, pivoting on the heels and keeping both feet parallel. Bend both knees, exhale slowly and sink your hips, lowering your entire body simultaneously raising the right heel, and bringing the Thermal Ruler down the middle of the left shin. (Take between six to eight seconds to reach this low position when you first do the exercise. With practice, you will later be able to expand your power and control to do the movement between twelve and fifteen seconds.) Now slowly inhale and straighten your legs, raising your back to the vertical position, simultaneously raising the left toes off the floor, and bringing the Thermal Ruler from the middle of the shin close to the body, to the level of the lower dantian two inches below the navel. Rise slowly, also taking six to eight seconds to complete the movement.

2. After you reach the complete upright position, shift and roll forward again and do another repetition of the cycle. Do a total

of four cycles on the left side. After the fourth repetition, pivot on both heels so that you face squarely to the front. Still holding the Thermal Ruler in the palms, take three resting/cleansing breaths. (Inhaling through the nose and exhaling through the mouth)

3. After the resting breaths, pivot 45 degrees to the right and repeat the cycle with four repetitions.

(Number of repetitions: four times on the left side, three cleansing breathes in the centered position, four times on the right side)

1

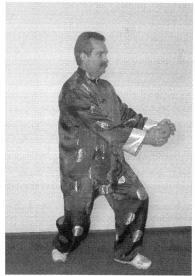

2

3

4

5

ADVANCED EXERCISE #2

1. Start with both feet parallel, pointing forward with a Thermal Ruler's distance between the heels. Turn both feet 45 degrees to the left, pivoting on the heels and keeping both feet parallel. Bend both knees, exhale slowly and sink your hips, lowering your entire body, simultaneously raising the right heel, and bringing the Thermal Ruler down the middle of the left shin. (Take between six to eight seconds to reach this low position when you first do the exercise. With practice, you will later be able to expand your power and control to do the movement between twelve and fifteen seconds.) Now slowly inhale and straighten your legs, raising your back to the vertical position, simultaneously raising the left toes off the floor, and bringing the Thermal Ruler from the middle of the shin close to the body, to the level of the middle dantian which is in the middle of the chest. Rise slowly, also taking six to eight seconds to complete the movement.

2. After you reach the complete upright position, shift and roll forward again and do another repetition of the cycle. Do a total

of eight cycles on the left side. After the eighth repetition, pivot on both heels so that you face squarely to the front. Still holding the Thermal Ruler in the palms, take three resting/cleansing breaths. (Inhaling through the nose and exhaling through the mouth)

3. After the resting breaths, pivot 45 degrees to the right and repeat the cycle with eight repetitions.

(Number of repetitions: eight times on the left side, three cleansing breathes, eight times on the right side)

1

2

3

4

4

6

7

ADVANCED EXERCISE #3

1. Start with both feet parallel, pointing forward with a Thermal Ruler's distance between the heels. Turn both feet 45 degrees to the left, pivoting on the heels and keeping both feet parallel. Bend both knees, exhale slowly and sink your hips, lowering your entire body, simultaneously raising the right heel, and bringing the Thermal Ruler down the middle of the left shin. (Take between six to eight seconds to reach this low position when you first do the exercise. With practice, you will later be able to expand your power and control to do the movement between twelve and fifteen seconds.) Now slowly inhale and straighten your legs, raising your back to the vertical position, simultaneously raising the left toes off the floor, and bringing the Thermal Ruler from the middle of the shin close to the body, to the level of the upper dantian located in the forehead. Rise slowly, also taking six to eight seconds to complete the movement.

2. After you reach the complete upright position, shift and roll forward again and do another repetition of the cycle. Do a total of eight cycles on the left side. After the eighth repetition, pivot

on both heels so that you face squarely to the front. Still holding the Thermal Ruler in the palms, take three resting/cleansing breaths. (Inhaling through the nose and exhaling through the mouth)

3. After the resting breaths, pivot 45 degrees to the right and repeat the cycle with eight repetitions.

(Number of repetitions: eight times on the left side, three cleansing breathes, eight times on the right side)

1

2

3

4

5

6

7   **8**

ADVANCED EXERCISE #4

Exercise four consists of eight steps forward and then eight steps back to the starting point, with the Thermal Ruler rolling through one orbit between the knee and the middle level dantian with each step.

1. Start by standing with feet together and holding the Thermal Ruler comfortably at thigh level. Face a direction that will allow you to move forward approximately twenty-five feet.

2. Slide your left foot forward, staying rooted in your right leg.

3. Then shift your weight forward, rolling the Thermal Ruler upward and outward at the level of the middle dantian. Continue the downward circling of the Thermal Ruler to knee level as you sit back onto the right leg.

4. With weight on the rear leg, turn the left foot to the left 45-degree, shift your weight forward over it (keeping the back vertical), and step forward straight ahead with the right foot. As you bring your weight onto the left leg, bring the Thermal Ruler slowly upward close along the torso to the approximate area of the middle dantian.

5. Then shift your weight from the left foot to the right, bringing the knee over the toes while rolling the Thermal Ruler upward, outward and then downwards towards the knee. As you circle the Thermal Ruler on its downward arc, shift back to the left leg and turn the right foot outward 45 degrees to the right.

6. Now take the third step, moving the left foot straight ahead, keeping your weight balanced on the right leg. Then shift your weight forward to the left leg, bringing the left knee over the toes, while rolling the Thermal Ruler forward. Continue this stepping and rolling action for five more repetitions to complete a total of eight steps. As you shift forward between each step, the action of the entire body is identical to the "Push" technique found in Taiji Quan.

7. After the eighth repetition you will have finished the right leg cycle. Pivot on the right toes and turn 180 degrees around to your left, facing the same direction that you just came from. Repeat the same cycle as before starting with the left foot. Continue this stepping and rolling action for eight more repetitions to complete this exercise.

8. After the eighth repetition you will have finished the right leg

cycle for the second time. Pivot on the right toes and turn 180 degrees around facing the same direction that you started from. Slide the left foot next to the right and perform a cleansing breath to finish this exercise.

1

2

2

4

5

ADVANCED EXERCISE #5

Exercise #5 is done in the traditional "horse riding" stance found in all Northern and internal styles of Chinese martial arts. Assume the "horse riding" stance by standing with your feet parallel and two shoulder widths apart.

1. This exercise is just like the #5 basic exercise, with the exception of a lower posture is used in the advanced exercise. Only after the practitioner has developed proficiency in the basic version should he or she attempt the advanced practice. In the advanced practice, the pattern of movement is the same as in the basic/beginner's level except that the entire "horse riding" stance is held lower so that the hips are at knee level and the Thermal Ruler is moved across from one knee to the other.

2. In the advanced practice of this exercise, gradually increase the duration of your exhalation from five seconds to fifteen seconds or more. Again, it is imperative that you remain fully relaxed as you do this exercise. This level of practice is achieved through regular training over a long period of time. There is no shortcut

in developing proficiency in this exercise-even for the most limber-for this exercise is performed with internal energy.

1   **2**

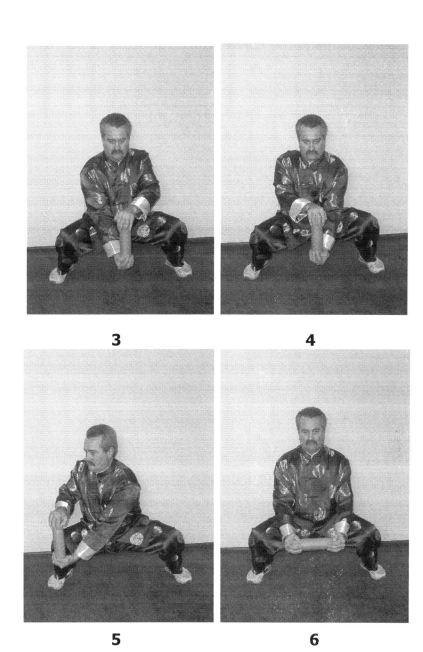

ADVANCED EXERCISE #6

Exercise #6 involves forward orbits of the Thermal Ruler, between knee level and the middle dantian level, done while stepping forward at 45 degree angles. This exercise is similar to the basic exercise #1, with the exception of the range of the orbit of the Thermal Ruler. This exercise moves four steps forwards and then turns and moves four steps back to the starting point.

1. Start with the feet together with at least fifteen feet of space in front of you. Sink your weight into the right leg and step out 45 degrees to the left with the left foot. Shift your weight forward and simultaneously lean the torso forward from the hips, extending the Thermal Ruler in an outward arc, down to the left knee; then shift the weight back to the right leg, bringing the Thermal Ruler in to the lower dantian level and raising the torso to vertical. You are now in a sit stance on your right leg. Continue the rolling action with the whole body and shift forward to the left leg again, bringing in the right leg alongside it and rolling the Thermal Ruler up from the lower dantian to the middle dantian.

2. Without stopping, turn your hips 90 degrees to the right and

step forward with the right foot to a 45-degree angle (right of the normal line), keeping your weight rooted in the left leg. As soon as you plant the right leg, shift your weight forward, lean forward rolling the Thermal Ruler outward and downward to just above the knee; then shift the weight back towards the left leg, raise the torso to the vertical and bring the Thermal Ruler in close to the lower dantian. Continue the rolling motion, shifting forward to the right leg and bringing the left leg alongside it while raising the Thermal Ruler to the middle dantian (solar plexus) level.

3. Without pausing, pivot the entire body 90 degrees to the left again, keeping the weight on the right leg. Slide the left foot out 45 degrees and continue with another orbit, moving the Thermal Ruler between the left knee and the middle dantian. Remember: when shifting forward, lean forward and roll the Thermal Ruler to knee level; when shifting backward, straighten the back to vertical and roll the Thermal Ruler from the knee up along the thigh, in close to the lower dantian, and up to the middle dantian.

4. After completing the third repetition, you are facing 45 degrees to

the left corner. Next, step to the right 45 degrees to the right corner. Slide the right foot forward and roll the Thermal Ruler forward and up to the middle dantian level. As the Thermal Ruler moves along its downward arc and comes into the body, turn the entire body to the left 180 degrees, pivoting on the ball of the right foot, and assume a sitting stance (the weight is 80% on the back leg) facing the direction from which you came. Shift your weight forward to the left leg as you roll out the Thermal Ruler once more 45 degrees to the left corner.

7. Continue with three more repetitions of this stepping/shifting movement.

8. The fourth and last repetition faces the starting Point and is done with the right foot forward. To end this cycle, as the Thermal Ruler moves along its downward arc and comes into the body, turn the entire body to the left 180 degrees, pivoting on the ball of the right foot, and assume a sitting stance facing the direction from which you came. Then raise the Thermal Ruler to the middle dantian level while drawing in the left foot alongside the right. Settle your weight equally on both feet, straighten both legs and simultaneously lower the Thermal Ruler from the middle dantian

level to the hips. This last cycle ends with an exhalation. You should be standing on the exact position on which you began, and you should be facing the same direction as you did in the beginning.

1

2

3

4

5

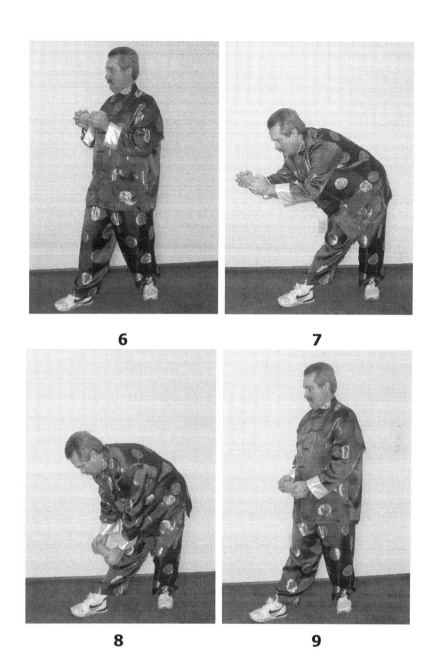

6

7

8

9

ADVANCED EXERCISE #7

Exercise #7 is done sitting on a table or a low ledge, with both feet suspended and hanging above the floor. Start from a rest position, holding the Thermal Ruler between the palms, resting it on the lap. This exercise performs eight repetitions at the lower dantian level, then eight at the middle dantian level, and finally eight at the upper dantian level (eye level). Between each level you must perform three cleansing breaths.

1. Inhale and raise the Thermal Ruler a few inches to the stomach level (lower dantian). Then exhale and carry the Thermal Ruler to the left side. Inhale and turn the Thermal Ruler to a vertical position with the left hand over the right. Keep the shoulders sunk and relaxed as you turn the Thermal Ruler.

2. Then slowly exhale and carry the Thermal Ruler across the body turning (rotating) the Thermal Ruler to the vertical position (right hand over left hand) as you pass the Thermal Ruler in from of the lower dantian. Continue to move the Thermal Ruler to the right side taking at least ten seconds to complete the pass. Inhale and carry the Thermal Ruler across the body turning the

Thermal Ruler to the vertical position (left hand over right hand) as you pass the Thermal Ruler in front of the lower dantian. Continue to move the Thermal Ruler to the left side taking at least ten seconds to complete the pass. Count this as one repetition.

3. After completing eight repetitions at the lower dantian level take three cleansing breaths facing straight ahead.

4. Continue this exercise as directed above, but for the next set pass the Thermal Ruler in front of the middle dantian level (solar plexus) for eight repetitions, then take three cleansing breaths facing straight ahead.

5. For the last set perform the exercise as directed above, but for the last set pass the Thermal Ruler in front of the upper dantian level (eye level) for eight repetitions, then conclude this exercise with three cleansing breaths.

Keep the shoulders relaxed throughout this exercise and breathe in through the nose and exhale out through the mouth.

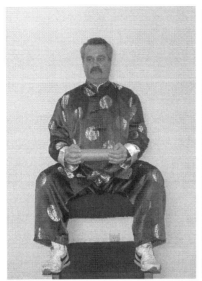

1

2

3

4

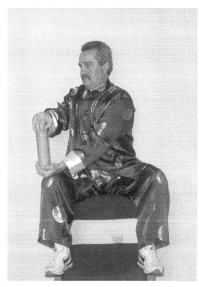

5

6

7

8

9

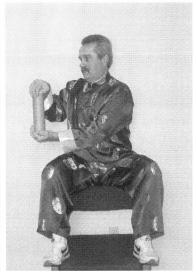

10

11

12

13

14

15

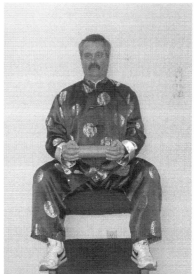
16

ADVANCED EXERCISE #8

Exercise #8 is performed lying down.

1. Lie down on your back with your knees bent or straight, and hold the Thermal Ruler over the lower dantian.

2. Then slowly turn the right end of the Thermal Ruler 45 degrees up from the line across your body (parallel to your waist line) so that the right hand is at your lowest rib on the right side and your left hand is down by the left hipbone. Take one deep inhale and exhale.

3. Now turn the Thermal Ruler 90 degrees in the other direction so that the left hand holding the Thermal Ruler is at your lowest rib on the left side and the right hand is down by the right hipbone. Take one deep inhale and exhale.

4. Return the Thermal Ruler to the lower dantian. Close the eyes. Raise the Thermal Ruler along the body up to eye level and continue rolling the Thermal Ruler outward (upward and inhale) away from the body and back down (exhale) to the lower

dantian. Do eight complete cycles of this exercise. After the eighth repetition, bring the Thermal Ruler to rest on the lower dantian, and complete one deep cleansing breath.

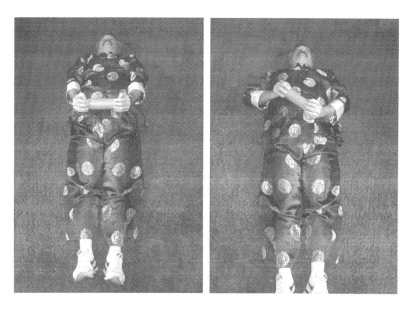

1   2

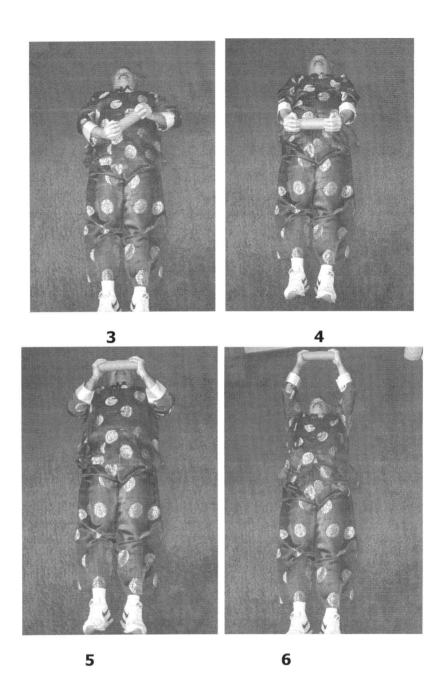

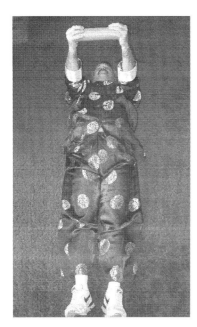 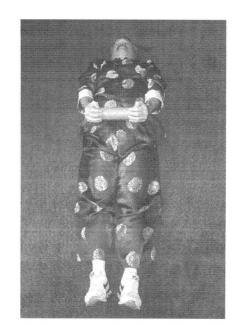

7 **8**

CONCLUSION

I hope that this book will get you started on the right path towards your development of better health and well-being. This book can be only a beginning of your practice. It is now up to you to experience the wonders of Qigong for yourself. The information in this book will enable you to lay a good foundation in the skills of energy development. I encourage you to seek out qualified instructors from which to learn.

Overall attitude creates positive self-fulfilling rewards. You have the power to influence your own future. First, you have to truly believe in those expectations so that your daily actions and decisions will begin to reflect them. Then, as if by magic, your expectations will come true. Your beliefs will shape your future. I hope you will benefit from the Dragonfly Qigong exercises as much as I have. Breathe deep and enjoy life to its fullest.

Dragonfly Wings

With wings beating like the beats of my heart,
life's great energy pulsates in and out
of every pore of my body.
Every breath I take comes into my soul,
the very essence of life itself.
To be a compassionate human being sets us apart,
with wings beating like the beats of my heart.

By, Dr. Michael Steward Sr.

Certified Dragonfly Qigong Instructors

Dr. Michael Steward Sr.
Dragonfly Tai-Chi/Qigong - Miami University Middletown Club
Miami University Continuing Education
4200 E. University Blvd.
Middletown, Ohio 45042-3497
513-727-3300
http://www.yamatanidojo.com/tai_chi_mainpage.htm
stewardm@infinet.com
513-317-7344

Dr. Michael Steward Sr.
Dragonfly Tai-Chi/Qigong - Miami University Oxford Club
Faith Lutheran Church Recreation Center
420 S. Campus Avenue
Oxford, Ohio
http://www.yamatanidojo.com/tai_chi_mainpage.htm
stewardm@infinet.com
513-317-7344

Dr. Michael Steward Sr.
Dragonfly Tai-Chi/Qigong – Quisno Wellness Center
Mt. Pleasant Retirement Village
Monroe, Ohio
http://www.yamatanidojo.com/tai_chi_mainpage.htm
stewardm@infinet.com
513-317-7344

Sifu Patrick Albrecht (Jiaoshi)
Dragonfly Tai-Chi/Qigong - Miami University Middletown Club
Miami University Continuing Education
4200 E. University Blvd.
Middletown, Ohio 45042-3497
513-727-3300
http://www.yamatanidojo.com/tai_chi_mainpage.htm
patrickah@ameritech.net

Sifu Patrick Albrecht (Jiaoshi)
Dragonfly Tai-Chi/Qigong - Miami University Oxford Club
Faith Lutheran Church Recreation Center
420 S. Campus Avenue
Oxford, Ohio
http://www.yamatanidojo.com/tai_chi_mainpage.htm
patrickah@ameritech.net

Sifu Patrick Albrecht (Jiaoshi)
Dragonfly Tai-Chi/Qigong – Quisno Wellness Center
Mt. Pleasant Retirement Village
Monroe, Ohio
http://www.yamatanidojo.com/tai_chi_mainpage.htm
patrickah@ameritech.net

(Sifu) Dr. James Barry MD (Jiaoshi)
Dragonfly Tai-Chi/Qigong - Miami University Middletown Club
Miami University Continuing Education
4200 E. University Blvd.
Middletown, Ohio 45042-3497
513-727-3300
http://www.yamatanidojo.com/tai_chi_mainpage.htm
docbarrylive@hotmail.com
937-746-1538

(Sifu) Dr. James Barry MD (Jiaoshi)
Dragonfly Tai-Chi/Qigong – Sycamore/Kettering Hospital Wellness Center
Miamisburg, Ohio
http://www.yamatanidojo.com/tai_chi_mainpage.htm
docbarrylive@hotmail.com
937-746-1538

(Sifu) Dr. James Barry MD (Jiaoshi)
Dragonfly Tai-Chi/Qigong – Otterbein Wellness Center
Otterbein Retirement Village
Lebanon, Ohio
http://www.yamatanidojo.com/tai_chi_mainpage.htm
docbarrylive@hotmail.com
937-746-1538

Sifu Christopher Dyszelski, MA (Jiaoshi)
Dragonfly Tai-Chi/Qigong - Miami University Oxford Club
Faith Lutheran Church Recreation Center
420 S. Campus Avenue
Oxford, Ohio
http://www.yamatanidojo.com/tai_chi_mainpage.htm
dyszelski@muohio.edu
513-664-4431

(Sifu) Dr. Tom Manson (Jiaoshi)
Dragonfly Tai-Chi/Qigong – Zheng Fu Tai-Chi/Qigong Club
Washington Courthouse, Ohio
http://www.yamatanidojo.com/tai_chi_mainpage.htm
tmaf@bright.net

(Sifu) Dr. Tom Manson (Jiaoshi)
Dragonfly Tai-Chi/Qigong – Zheng Fu Tai-Chi/Qigong Club
Chillicothe, Ohio
http://www.yamatanidojo.com/tai_chi_mainpage.htm
tmaf@bright.net

(Sifu) Jim Karnes (Jiaoshi)
Dragonfly Tai-Chi/Qigong – Collegeville Tai-Chi/Qigong Club
Collegeville, Penn.
http://www.yamatanidojo.com/tai_chi_mainpage.htm
RangerJMK@aol.com

James Stubbles, Fu Jiao Lien
Dragonfly Tai-Chi/Qigong - Miami University Middletown Club
Miami University Continuing Education
4200 E. University Blvd.
Middletown, Ohio 45042-3497
513-727-3300
http://www.yamatanidojo.com/tai_chi_mainpage.htm
Jim_Stubbles@msn.com
937-748-9815

Dennis Kelly, Fu Jiao Lien
Dragonfly Tai-Chi/Qigong - Miami University Middletown Club
Miami University Continuing Education
4200 E. University Blvd.
Middletown, Ohio 45042-3497
513-727-3300
http://www.yamatanidojo.com/tai_chi_mainpage.htm
Dgkelly5@aol.com

Josh Toms, Fu Jiao Lien
Dragonfly Tai-Chi/Qigong - Miami University Middletown Club
Miami University Continuing Education
4200 E. University Blvd.
Middletown, Ohio 45042-3497
513-727-3300
http://www.yamatanidojo.com/tai_chi_mainpage.htm
Stoms@cinci.rr.com

ISBN 141200335-0

Made in the USA
Lexington, KY
02 February 2012